C000054403

Pearson Edexcel GCSE (9–1)

History

Mao's China, 1945–76

Revision Guide and Workbook

Series Consultant: Harry Smith

Author: Rob Bircher

A note from the publisher

In order to ensure that this resource offers high-quality support for the associated Pearson qualification, it has been through a review process by the awarding body. This process confirms that this resource fully covers the teaching and learning content of the specification or part of a specification at which it is aimed. It also confirms that it demonstrates an appropriate balance between the development of subject skills, knowledge and understanding, in addition to preparation for assessment.

Endorsement does not cover any guidance on assessment activities or processes (e.g. practise questions or advice on how to answer assessment questions), included in the resource nor does it prescribe any particular approach to the teaching or delivery of a related course.

While the publishers have made every attempt to ensure that advice on the qualification and its assessment is accurate, the official specification and associated assessment guidance materials are the only authoritative source of information and should always be referred to for definitive guidance.

Pearson examiners have not contributed to any sections in this resource relevant to examination papers for which they have responsibility.

Examiners will not use endorsed resources as a source of material for any assessment set by Pearson.

Endorsement of a resource does not mean that the resource is required to achieve this Pearson qualification, nor does it mean that it is the only suitable material available to support the qualification, and any resource lists produced by the awarding body shall include this and other appropriate resources.

For the full range of Pearson revision titles across KS2, 11+, KS3, GCSE, Functional Skills, AS/A Level and BTEC visit:
www.pearsonschools.co.uk/revise

Contents

SUBJECT CONTENT

Establishing communist rule, 1945–59

The Civil War, 1945–49

1   China in 1945

2   The Civil War

Communist rule

3   Mao Zedong

4   The CCP

The CCP, 1951–52

5   The use of terror

6   The 'antis' movements

The Hundred Flowers campaign, 1956–57

7   Hundred Flowers: reasons

8   Hundred Flowers: features and results

Economic policy, 1949–65

Agricultural changes, 1949–57

9   Land reform

10 Cooperation and collectivisation

The communes

11 Communal living

12 The great famine

Industry, 1953–57

13 The first Five-Year Plan

14 Plan successes and failures

Industry, 1958–65

15 The Great Leap Forward

16 Economic reform

The Cultural Revolution and its aftermath, 1966–76

Cultural Revolution: reasons

17 The Cultural Revolution

18 Purification of communism

Red Guards, Red Terror

19 Student rebellion

20 Red Terror

Cultural Revolution: effects

21 Political effects

22 Social and economic effects

Cultural Revolution: end

23 Winding down

24 The Gang of Four

Life in Mao's China, 1949–76

Communist control

25 Propaganda and censorship

26 Thought control

Family life and women

27 Changes in family life

28 Changes for women

Education and health

29 Changes in education

30 Changes in health provision

Cultural change

31 Attacks on traditional culture

32 Attacks on religion

SKILLS

33 Exam overview

34 Sources and interpretations

35 Question 1: Making inferences

36 Question 2: Explaining causes

37 Question 3(a): Evaluating usefulness

38 Question 3(b): Identifying and explaining differences

39 Question 3(c): Suggesting reasons for different views

40 Question 3(d) Evaluating interpretations

41 Sources/Interpretations Booklet

42 PRACTICE

56 ANSWERS

. . . .

A small bit of small print

Edexcel publishes Sample Assessment Material and the Specification on its website. This is the official content and this book should be used in conjunction with it. The questions in *Now try this* have been written to help you practise every topic in the book. Remember: the real exam questions may not look like this.

China in 1945

1945 saw the start of the Chinese Civil War. Chiang Kai-shek's Guomindang (GMD), the Nationalist Party, was in a much stronger position than Mao Zedong's Communist Party (CCP). This page looks at their relative strengths and weaknesses.

GMD: strengths and weaknesses

Strengths	Weaknesses
• Some popular support for overseeing China's victory in 1945 against Japan in the Second World War.	• Bad working conditions in factories meant the GMD lost support from workers.
• Control of China's cities, which meant control of factories, including weapons factories.	• Government corruption and the introduction of censorship made the GMD unpopular.
• The official government, which meant aid from other countries – especially the USA, which was Japan's enemy and which also wanted to limit the spread of communism and the influence of its rival, the USSR.	• Refusing calls for land reform meant the GMD lost support from peasants.
• Strategic position: controlled China's densely populated areas – 75 per cent of its population.	• Poor GMD economic policies led to unemployment and inflation.
• 2.5 million soldiers – the GMD's army was twice as big as Mao's People's Liberation Army (PLA).	• A failure to address women's rights meant the GMD lost support from many women.

The USA wanted China on its (capitalist) side to counter the USSR.

As time went on, popular support for the GMD declined.

CCP: strengths and weaknesses

The CCP was in a much weaker position than the GMD in 1945. It had fewer and less well-equipped troops, no aircraft and few cities. But it had four key advantages that increased as the GMD weakened.

1. The CCP supported land reform. This was important because it meant that peasants supported it.

2. The USSR supported the CCP because of their shared communist ideas. For example, in 1945 the USSR allowed the PLA to take 100 000 guns abandoned in Manchuria by the Japanese.

3. Strategic position: the CCP controlled rural northern China (the countryside). This gave it a strong base and meant it could influence the population of a whole region.

4. Tactics: the CCP's army, the PLA, were very experienced **guerrilla** fighters (from fighting the Japanese). Their fighters could hide among the rural population, then launch surprise attacks.

The CCP was communist **and also** nationalist: it wanted an independent China, too.

Key terms

Civil war – when groups of people from the same country fight each other in order to gain political control.

Land reform – sharing out farmland so that more people have more land, rather than just a few people owning almost all the land.

Censorship – controls on what the media can say, usually to reduce criticism of the government.

Communist – someone who believes in a completely equal society where no one owns anything and everyone works for the benefit of everyone else.

Nationalist – someone who believes their country should be independent and run to benefit its people.

Make sure you know what these key terms mean, and use them in your answers.

Turn to page 2 to see how these strengths and weaknesses affected the course of the war.

Now try this

Give **three** reasons why the USA supported the Guomindang (GMD) rather than the CCP.

The Civil War

Mao's leadership and the increasing unpopularity of the GMD meant the CCP's People's Liberation Army (PLA) went from near-destruction in May 1947 to victory in October 1949 in the Civil War.

Manchuria and the GMD

In August 1945, Soviet troops invaded Manchuria to defeat the Japanese. This was a threat to the GMD because Soviet troops might help the CCP across the border.

Chiang made a deal with the USSR to prevent the CCP gaining control. In November 1945, the USA flew 110000 GMD troops into the region to take over. By May 1947, the GMD controlled all but one of the northern cities.

Why was Manchuria significant?

By November 1948, the GMD had lost Manchuria to the PLA. This was significant because:

- Manchuria was rich with modern industry and the Japanese occupiers had left large stocks of weapons there.
- Corruption made the GMD unpopular with Manchurians, but the CCP's support for land reform made it very popular. This brought more people onto the CCP's side – by October 1948, 1.6 million peasants had joined the PLA.
- GMD troops and equipment were trapped in northern cities and were captured by the PLA.
- The GMD had committed so much to Manchuria that it lost a third of all its troops.

What was the Huai-Hai Campaign?

The Huai-Hai Campaign was the last major battle of the Civil War. The GMD had 800000 troops, 200000 more than the PLA. But the PLA also had 600000 guerrilla fighters and 1 million peasants supporting it.

The campaign lasted from 6 November 1948 to 10 January 1949. The PLA won.

Three impacts of Huai-Hai

Huai-Hai was a turning point in the Civil War.

- Morale among GMD troops was low – thousands deserted to join the PLA.
- By January 1949, the GMD had lost 500000 troops. Now it had no way to stop the PLA's advance into southern China.
- Chiang resigned after the PLA won the Huai-Hai Campaign.

Reasons for the CCP's success in the Civil War

Reasons for CCP success: Peasant support	Reasons for CCP success: Leadership
• Peasants wanted land. The CCP gave land; the GMD blocked land reform. • Peasants fed the PLA, helped to transport supplies for it and fought alongside it. • Mao speeded up land reform and made sure the PLA treated peasants well.	• Mao had ordered PLA troops to retreat. His decision meant that the PLA kept its military strength despite defeats. • Chiang did nothing to stop government corruption and he opposed land reform. This reduced support for the GMD.
Reasons for CCP success: Economic factors	Reasons for CCP success: Strategy
• Unemployment and inflation due to GMD policies made it unpopular and led to unrest in the cities. • High unemployment and inflation meant many strikes in GMD-controlled cities. The CCP helped organise these strikes.	• Mao worked well with his generals and this meant the PLA could act quickly. • Chiang disagreed with some of his generals, causing military confusion. • Guerrilla tactics helped preserve PLA forces and minimise GMD strengths.

Now try this

Explain why Mao's leadership was important in achieving victory in the Civil War. Give **three** reasons.

Mao Zedong

Mao was the leader of the CCP because of his successful strategies, his vision for a strong China and his ideas. This gave the CCP its **ideology** (the political beliefs that guided its actions).

Reasons for Mao's authority within the CCP

Mao held a dominant position because:

- he had led the CCP through long years of hardship and the CCP trusted his leadership
- his guerrilla tactics against Japan and the GMD meant the PLA survived, so he had the army's backing
- he worked well with other leading CCP and PLA leaders, who therefore supported him
- he showed how **Marxism** could apply to peasants
- his nationalism made him popular with non-Marxists as well. At first, his government was democratic, including representatives from many different political views.

This photo of Mao shows him dressed in a PLA-like military uniform, reflecting his authority in the Party and in the army.

Marxism

Karl Marx believed society was heading towards a time of communal living and equality – **communism** – that would see the workers freeing themselves from Western capitalist society.

Mao's ideology

Nationalism	The power of the peasants
Mao was a Marxist, but also a nationalist. He argued that: • China had to unite to resist attempts to enslave its people • because China had been treated badly by the West in the past, China needed to combat the West and its capitalism • China had been a world power for most of its long history, until the West made it poor. It was time for China to 'stand up'.	Marx had said only urban workers could lead a communist revolution. China had few urban workers – 80 per cent of China's population were peasants. Mao applied Marxism to peasants: • He said that, because the peasants would benefit from communism, they could support a revolution led by communists. • Mao believed mobilising China's millions of peasants would make China unbeatable. • This mass mobilisation of peasants would form a revolutionary army. Guerrilla tactics meant untrained peasants could often win against trained soldiers in the countryside. • Mass mobilisation of China's huge population would also help to counteract the greater industrial power of China's rivals.

Mao's leadership in the 1940s

In the 1930s, Mao had worked out his military and political theories. He argued against other CCP leaders who wanted to follow the way the USSR worked. As a nationalist, Mao believed that China could find its own path.

In 1943, Mao became the leader of the CCP. He ordered a **purge** of the CCP – this meant getting rid of anyone who disagreed with his ideas. More than 10 000 people were killed. The CCP officially took on Mao's ideas as their ideology.

Mao and the 'people's war'

Mao developed the idea of the 'people's war'. Instead of trying to build a Western-style regular army, his military theory said that:

- really strong motivation made people better fighters than having advanced weapons
- if fighters treated local peasants well, the peasants would support them
- even if outnumbered, enemy armies could be worn down with ambushes.

Now try this

Write a paragraph to explain why Mao needed to adapt Marxism in order to make it fit with China's situation.

The CCP

Mao set up a democratic government for the People's Republic of China (PRC) in 1949, but it was soon dominated by the CCP. Mao took control of all the key leading roles in government.

China's new government

At first, the government of the new PRC was very democratic. The 1954 **constitution** set out how China would be governed. It included:

- equal rights, multi-party elections and free speech
- a parliament to make laws: the National People's Congress
- Provisional Congresses to govern China's provinces and main cities
- a State Council, elected by the National People's Congress, that was in charge of the government ministries and decision-making
- a premier (prime minister) of the State Council. The first premier was **Zhou Enlai**.

The role of the CCP

The CCP was too small to govern China on its own at first, which meant working with people from other political parties. But, as the party grew, the CCP took control. By the end of 1952, the CCP dominated government decisions and actions.

New mass party membership

The CCP grew from 4.5 million members in 1949 to 6.5 million in 1953.
Mao used mass Party membership to organise mass campaigns, for example the 'antis' movements, which were very important in helping the CCP secure control of China.

For more on the 'antis' movements, see page 6.

Democratic centralism

The CCP was a very disciplined political organisation. The central leadership kept tight control of China's government policy.

However, it did also give Party members the right to take part in discussions about policy and to vote (in a controlled way) on what policies should be. The Party saw this as democracy.

Once a decision was made, discussion stopped and everyone in the Party had a duty to carry it out. This was called **democratic centralism**.

The 1954 constitution

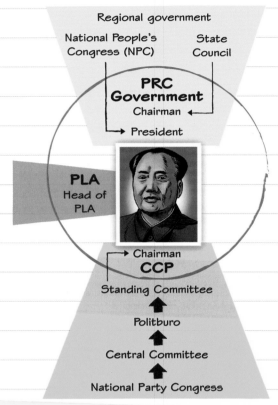

Regional government

National People's Congress (NPC)   State Council

PRC Government
Chairman

President

PLA
Head of PLA

Chairman
CCP

Standing Committee

Politburo

Central Committee

National Party Congress

Mao held all of the key roles in the government and controlled the army. His views were the basis of Party policy and he effectively picked the members of the Politburo and the Standing Committee, and PLA generals.

Organisation of the CCP

- CCP members met in Regional Congresses. A National Congress of regional delegates elected the Central Committee, but the elections were tightly controlled by the Party.
- A small group of Central Committee members, called the Politburo, decided what the Party would do.
- The Politburo was powerful, but its Standing Committee was more powerful (although Mao could still make decisions without it). Zhou Enlai was a senior member and was responsible for making sure Party policy was carried out.
- The first chairman of the Standing Committee was **Liu Shaoqi**.

Now try this

Mao Zedong, Zhou Enlai and Liu Shaoqi were the three most important men in the PRC in the 1950s. Write short paragraphs to describe each man's role in governing the People's Republic of China (PRC).

The use of terror

Mao used terror to remove people who might challenge the CCP for control of China.

Political classification

After the Civil War ended, the CCP gave everyone in China a 'class label'. 'Red' categories were 'friends of the revolution' and 'black' categories were 'enemies of the revolution'.

Black categories included:	Red categories included:
• Landlords • Richer peasants • Counter-revolutionaries • 'Bad-influencers' (for example, criminals) • 'Rightists' (supporters of capitalism)	• Poorer peasants • Workers • Soldiers of the PLA • Families of PLA soldiers • Revolutionary activists

Attacks on landlords, 1950

The CCP speeded up the process of land reform by attacking landlords who refused to hand their land over to the peasants.

- Whole villages were encouraged by the PLA to turn against their landlords. Mass meetings were held in which peasants 'spoke bitterness' against landlords.
- Landlords were fined, had their land, houses and possessions confiscated, were beaten and were expelled from villages.
- At least 1 million landlords were killed, possibly many more, and 40 per cent of China's farmland was seized by peasants.

Campaign to suppress 'counter revolutionaries', 1951

This targeted possible opponents in the cities, who were accused of being spies and criminals.

- Many different activities were counted as 'counter-revolutionary crimes', including any collaboration with the old GMD government.
- People were accused of being counter-revolutionaries at mass public meetings. Many were sentenced to death.
- An estimated 2 per cent of the urban population was targeted, with thousands killed.
- The CCP also banned groups that might challenge them, and attacked religious leaders.

Punishment of offenders

The terror was designed to be very public. Mao and other senior CCP leaders wanted the punishments to be 'educational' so that people would learn the CCP was in control.

- People were tortured to get them to confess to crimes.
- Large meetings were held in which people were publicly accused and forced to make humiliating confessions.
- If people were sentenced to death, the executions were often carried out at the same meetings, in front of the crowds.
- Many were sentenced to hard labour in prison camps. Conditions were harsh: in one prison mine, 300 people died per day.
- Others lost their property or were fined.

Role of the Chinese people

Mao's view was that, as long as terror campaigns targeted unpopular individuals, the Chinese people would support the campaigns.

- Mao wanted his terror campaigns to be mass movements. The public trials and executions were advertised in newspapers and on the radio. There were huge crowds for many of the trials and public executions.
- Ordinary people played an important role in making accusations against landlords and other 'counter-revolutionaries'. Sometimes people did this to settle old scores.
- Although the public seemed to support the terror, most people were terrified. There were thousands of suicides by people who were worried they might be accused of something.

Now try this

In a paragraph, explain why CCP leaders saw the use of punishment during the terror as being 'educational'.

The 'antis' movements

Terror was used to remove possible opposition to CCP control and no one was sure how far Mao would go. The **'antis' movements** extended CCP domination of China's government and economy.

The 'three antis' movement, 1951

The 'three antis' movement was called *Sanfan*. It targeted CCP officials who had links to the old GMD government – which meant loyal CCP members could replace them. Mao encouraged the Chinese people to clean the 'filth and poison' left over from the old government of China.

Mao launched *Sanfan* to deal with three problems with government:

Corruption — **Sanfan** — Waste

Government inefficiency (bureaucracy)

Bureaucracy

A **bureaucracy** is where a group of officials is employed to do the work of government. The word can be used as a criticism of inefficient government when bureaucracy has become a complicated official system that is annoying or confusing because it has a lot of rules and processes: 'red tape'.

Consequences of *Sanfan*

- 4 million people were investigated: 1 million were either sent to labour camps or executed.
- The campaign caused major problems for government. For example, tax did not get collected in some areas.
- These problems meant Mao was forced to end *Sanfan* after one month.

There was a close connection between *Sanfan* and *Wufan*: *Sanfan* was about getting rid of CCP officials who had been corrupted by capitalism. *Wufan* was a direct attack on capitalism in China. The campaigns both weakened the power of the bureaucracy, which had been very strong in China for centuries, and cleared the way for a new generation of Mao supporters.

The 'five antis' movement, 1952

The 'five antis' movement was called *Wufan*. It targeted the wealthy Chinese capitalists who ran industry. Businesses were raided and investigated by the CCP, who were looking for any evidence of wrongdoing.

The CCP made sure everyone was aware of the *Wufan* campaign. Propagandists visited businesses and encouraged workers to criticise their bosses.

The 'five antis' focused on five key problems in industry. They also aimed to stamp out 'capitalist thinking' in China.

Consequences of *Wufan*

Bribery — Theft of government property — **Wufan** — Theft of government secrets — Fraud — Tax evasion

- Almost all of China's major companies were investigated: 450 000 companies.
- Although only 1 per cent of those put on trial went to prison, many were fined. The fines were so large that many companies went bankrupt and were taken over by the government.
- As a result, the government received a lot of money in fines, and had a stronger hold on the economy from owning the companies.
- Business leaders were very frightened by the campaign. This made them much more likely to do what the government told them.
- Workers supported the campaigns, which meant more support for the CCP. The CCP increased its control over China's government and its economy.

Now try this

Suggest **two** ways in which the 'antis' movements helped consolidate Mao's control over China.

Hundred Flowers: reasons

In 1956, after successes in consolidating the CCP's control over China, Mao encouraged scientists, artists and writers to criticise the Chinese Communist Party in the Hundred Flowers campaign. By mid-1957, this increasingly free and open campaign was clearly over.

1 Unrest in European communist countries (for example, Hungary and Poland, 1956) following Soviet leader Stalin's death in 1953.

2 Soviet leader Khrushchev's 'secret speech' in the USSR in 1956 criticised Stalin's use of terror against Communist Party members and suggested a more liberal approach would be encouraged.

Khrushchev believed very strongly in communism as the best possible political system. He was sure that people would come together to make the system work better.

Reasons for the Hundred Flowers campaign: international

3 Communist parties began experimenting with increasing free speech in politics and reducing central control of the economy. They hoped to re-connect the workers to communism, and help iron out the growth of too much unpopular bureaucracy within Communist parties.

Mao's slogan, 'Let a hundred flowers blossom, let a hundred schools of thought contend' gave rise to numerous propaganda images involving flowers.

It is possible that the Hundred Flowers campaign was a trap for opponents of the regime. This is certainly what many in the CCP suspected. However, Mao did not give this as a reason.

1 Mao's suspicion of experts and bureaucrats. He feared the CCP was becoming bureaucratic, inefficient and corrupt. The Party was in danger of being an out-of-touch, privileged elite and a barrier to further developments. Mao wanted this reformed through criticism.

2 Mao's desire to listen to the grievances of ordinary people and hear how they thought the CCP could be improved. He still believed firmly in mobilising the masses.

Reasons for the Hundred Flowers campaign: domestic

6 A series of strikes throughout 1956, with workers demanding better pay, suggested that CCP officials were misbehaving and serving their own interests rather than those of the people.

3 Mao's growing confidence in the benefits of communism and expectations that freer speech would therefore mean praise for the regime, and its economic and military achievements. Mao was confident that people supported communism and that terror had wiped out many opponents.

5 In order to industrialise China, the CCP needed the support of China's technical experts and academics. As the economy recovered from the Civil War, plans to develop new factories, power stations and infrastructure (bridges, roads, canals) needed their expertise.

See page 13 for Mao's attempts to industrialise China in the Five-Year Plans.

4 Mao's desire to assert his domination of the Party and strengthen his own position by allowing criticism of the CCP. He expected that the people would use free expression to praise him for his successes (making him stronger), but criticise ways in which the Party was not meeting their socialist needs (making rivals in charge of government ministries weaker).

Now try this

Think about how the campaign encouraged freer speech.

1 Explain what Mao meant by his slogan, 'Let a hundred flowers blossom'.
2 'The main reason for the Hundred Flowers campaign was that Mao was concerned that Party officials had become disconnected from ordinary people.' Suggest **two** points that could be used to challenge this interpretation.

Hundred Flowers: features and results

The Hundred Flowers campaign went through several different stages in the years 1956–57. The reaction of Mao and the CCP to the campaign also changed – from support, to concern, to a crack-down.

Main stages of the campaign

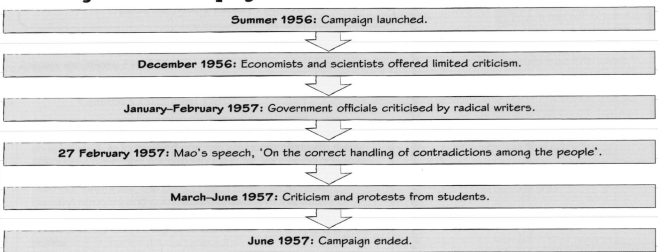

Summer 1956: Campaign launched.

December 1956: Economists and scientists offered limited criticism.

January–February 1957: Government officials criticised by radical writers.

27 February 1957: Mao's speech, 'On the correct handling of contradictions among the people'.

March–June 1957: Criticism and protests from students.

June 1957: Campaign ended.

Key features of the campaign

- Mao launched the campaign by inviting criticism of certain aspects of the CCP, including administration. He did not want criticism of politics, however.
- At first (December 1956), criticism was very limited, but it became stronger. This was the period of 'blooming and contending' when Mao still supported the criticism.
- In January and February, radical writers criticised the CCP for corruption and bureaucracy. This was unpopular with the CCP, but Mao continued to support it.
- On 27 February, Mao gave a famous speech about resolving 'contradictions', but gave no indication of what might be acceptable.
- In March–June 1957, students began to criticise politics, calling for free elections. They published their own newspapers, which the CCP could not control. Some criticised Mao's use of terror.
- By June 1957, the students had run away with the campaign. Mao now claimed the aim had actually been to 'let poisonous weeds sprout and grow', to identify and root out these counter-revolutionaries.
- Mao ended the campaign and the 'Anti-Rightist' purge began.

Results of the Hundred Flowers campaign

- Instead of the expected praise and constructive feedback, the CCP came increasingly under attack from students and others.
- Mao's response was a terror campaign like the 'antis' movements – the 'Anti-Rightist' purge of 1957–59.
- Intellectuals and students who had spoken out against the CCP were humiliated and forced to confess in public mass meetings. Between 300 000 and 500 000 people were sent to prison labour camps for 're-education'.
- Because ordinary people had not praised the CCP and communism as expected, educational programmes were set up for workers and peasants. This was so they could learn to appreciate the CCP.
- Mao blamed 'bureaucratic elements' in the CCP for making the CCP unpopular. Between 5 and 10 per cent of the top CCP officials were removed.
- Zhou Enlai publicly apologised for failing to put Mao's economic policies into action fast enough. This strengthened Mao's position.
- Mao also became stronger because people assumed the Hundred Flowers campaign was a deliberate trap to help purge the CCP.

Now try this

1 Explain what Mao meant when he referred to 'poisonous weeds'.
2 List **three** ways in which the results of the Hundred Flowers campaign strengthened Mao's position.

Land reform

Mao's early agricultural policies (1949–57) were successful – agricultural production increased. Breaking up landlord control and giving peasants more land also made these policies very popular.

Features of land reform

- The CCP had already started land reform in northern provinces during the Civil War. Now the Party extended it across China.
- The Agrarian Reform Law of 1950 gave the CCP the legal right to take land from landlords and **redistribute** it to peasants.
- From December 1951, the CCP began setting up agricultural cooperatives.
- Between 1950 and 1952, 40 per cent of China's farmland had been redistributed and 60 per cent of peasants gained more land.

The CCP slogan for land reform was 'land to the tiller'. A **tiller** is the person actually farming the land. Previously, peasants rented land from landlords, which kept them poor and under the landlords' control.

Reasons for land reform

- **Political**: landlords were often GMD supporters and certainly never supported the CCP. Land reform helped get rid of political opponents of the CCP.
- **Political**: land reform was very popular with peasants. Peasant support was essential for control of the People's Republic of China.
- **Ideological**: communists claimed the renting system exploited peasants and created inequality, and that communism would lead to an equal society without exploitation.
- **Economic**: more land and the **four freedoms** gave peasants reasons to improve farming. This was important because China needed to increase farming efficiency in order to promote industrial development and feed the increasing urban workforce.

Land reform and terror

Landlords were a 'Black Category' class. Attacks on landlordism were part of Mao's use of terror.

- ☑ Peasants were encouraged by the CCP to seize land from landlords.
- ☑ Landlords were forced into humiliating public confessions of guilt in '**struggle meetings**'.
- ☑ Landlords were frequently killed in the land reform process or lost everything.

See page 5 for more on the terror. You can learn more about 'struggle meetings' on page 26.

Features of cooperation

Mao and the CCP saw land reform as a first step to **collectivising** agriculture.

- ☑ Small farms were not as efficient as large farms, which could afford machinery.
- ☑ Small farms were not socialist. Marxism taught that individual farmers were always drawn towards capitalism.
- ☑ Small farms would not help industrialisation. Mao needed control over food prices so workers' wages did not need to be high.

See page 10 for more on collectivisation.

The Four Freedoms

The Four Freedoms were as important as redistributing land because they gave peasants good reasons to improve their land, increase the amount they produced and increase the amount they sold (traded) for profit.

Between 1950 and 1952, agricultural production increased by 15 per cent a year.

The freedom to trade (sell products at market)

The freedom to buy, sell and rent land

What were the Four Freedoms?

The freedom to lend money to others

The freedom to hire labour (workers)

Now try this

List **three** reasons why land reform was a success for Mao and the CCP.

Cooperation and collectivisation

Between 1951 and 1957, Mao and the CCP introduced changes in agriculture which they believed would encourage peasant farmers to work cooperatively: sharing tools, land and labour. **Collective farming** meant large-scale, state-owned farms, organised on socialist principles.

Agricultural policy, 1950–57

Timeline

1950 Agrarian Reform Law

1951 Mutual Aid Teams (MATs) introduced

1953 Agricultural Producers' Cooperatives (APCs) introduced

1955 Advanced Agricultural Producers' Cooperatives introduced

1956 Record harvests achieved

1957 Almost 90 per cent of peasants had joined Advanced APCs.

Gradual changes in farming

- Small farms were inefficient while large farms could be worked efficiently by machinery.
- Marxist theory aimed for collective farming so that all farms were equal.
- Peasant support was essential to the CCP so changes were gradual and voluntary.
- In the USSR, Stalin had used terror to force **collectivisation** on peasants, causing unrest and famine. This made Mao more cautious.

Successes by 1957

Land reform convinced the majority of peasants that the CCP was on their side:

- By the end of 1952, around 40 per cent of peasants had voluntarily joined MATs.
- But APCs went too far for most peasants: only 14 per cent had joined one in 1955.
- Widespread flooding in 1954 caused grain shortages in 1955. The CCP put heavy pressure on peasants to join collectives.
- By 1957, almost 90 per cent of peasants were in Advanced APCs. Food production increased by 40 per cent in 1951–57.

Growth of MATs: key features

Mutual Aid Teams (MATs) were the first step in encouraging peasants to move to more cooperative ways of farming.

- MATs were promoted from 1951 to 1952.
- A MAT was a group of peasant households (between five and ten) that worked as a team for big farming jobs, like planting and harvesting.
- The peasants in the MAT shared tools and equipment, making farming more efficient.
- Peasants still owned their own land.
- MATs were voluntary and peasants could join or leave at any time.

Growth of APCs: key features

- Agricultural Producers' Cooperatives (APCs) were promoted in 1953–55.
- APCs involved larger numbers of households (usually 20–30 households) putting all their land and resources together.
- This created larger fields, which could be farmed more efficiently using machinery.
- Each APC member was paid according to how much work they did. Members were also paid according to how much land and other resources they contributed.
- APCs were voluntary and households could leave them and still keep their land.

Advanced APCs: key features

Advanced APCs created large-scale farms that operated in a socialist way:

- Advanced APCs were promoted in 1955–56.
- They were large (150–200 households). This often meant combining several villages.
- Now people were only paid according to the amount of work they did rather than how much land was contributed. This equality was an important principle of socialism.
- Advanced APCs were voluntary, too. Households could leave them and keep their property.

Now try this

State **one** reason why Mao and the CCP did not force collectivisation on peasants in the period 1949–57.

Communal living

In 1958, huge collective farms – **communes** – were introduced as part of the **Great Leap Forward**. This was a rapid acceleration in communist agricultural policy and a radical change for peasants.

> The Great Leap Forward (1958–62) was Mao's second 'Five-Year Plan' for industrialising China. Turn to page 15 to find out more.

The impact of the Great Leap Forward

Instead of the gradual, voluntary change in agriculture (1951–57), in 1958 Mao insisted on radical change. Reasons for this included:

- Mao worried that bureaucratic Party rules were crushing revolutionary spirit.

> In 1958, the CCP introduced enforced collectivisation. This meant that collectivisation became compulsory.

- Mao wanted China to industrialise rapidly. This required large-scale, modern, efficient farms to produce plenty of food to feed industrial workers.
- One slogan of the Great Leap Forward was 'politics in charge'. Mao believed the Chinese people could achieve anything.

Lysenkoism: nature and impact

Trofim Lysenko was an agricultural scientist from the USSR. He developed new socialist approaches to farming that, he said, would rapidly increase crop yields.

Following his ideas was called 'Lysenkoism'. The CCP introduced Lysenkoism for the communes to follow.

Lysenkoism was based on the idea that harsh conditions created stronger crops. To challenge crops to become stronger, Lysenko advised that:

- seeds should be stored in cold, damp conditions (instead of cool, dry conditions)
- seeds should be planted very deeply and close together.

Lysenkoism imagined a perfect world, but was not based on reliable evidence.

Communist science

Although Lysenkoism appears ridiculous now, at the time Chinese communists believed that different rules applied in communist countries, even in science, because communism was superior in every way to capitalism.

> Communes were organised so that every aspect of people's lives was controlled.

Organisation of the communes

- The communes were very large: most had around 5000 households.
- Communal living was compulsory – by the end of 1958, about 400 million people were organised into over 26 500 communes: amazingly rapid change.
- People had to give up all their land and resources to the commune, as private farming was abolished. They worked for the commune now, not for themselves.
- The commune worked in a military way. Families were organised into work teams, and work teams were organised into brigades. Brigades were given specific jobs to do. Each work team then had its specific role and its own targets to meet.
- There was a mix of agricultural and industrial work, not just farming; for example, making steel in backyard furnaces. Communes also worked together to build irrigation channels.
- Schools, childcare and care for old people were provided so adults could work.
- Food and healthcare were provided freely to all commune members, as much as they needed: an important communist principle.
- Everyone between 15 and 50 was in the commune's militia and had military training.
- The commune's police (made up from the militia) monitored everyone and punished those who did not do what they were supposed to do for the commune.
- The CCP monitored each commune and Party members made sure all decisions made by the commune were in line with CCP policy.

Now try this

Describe **three** features of communal living that helped to make communes productive.

The great famine

The great famine of 1958–62 led to as many as 30 million deaths across China. The impact lasted for decades. There are different theories about what caused the famine.

Impact of bad weather, 1959–61

Communes:
• Disruption caused by backyard furnaces

Possible causes of the great famine

Consequences of government policy:
• Lysenkoism
• Four Pests Campaign

Mao's radical ideology

Familiarise yourself with the different interpretations of the causes of the great famine.

See pages 14–16 for more on Mao's radical ideology.

Impacts of the great famine

• **Social:** tens of millions of people died.
• **Social:** breakdown in order as peasants tried to take grain from commune stores. Those caught were executed without trial.
• **Social and political:** communes fell apart in famine regions as people struggled to keep their families alive.
• **Political:** Mao lost authority in the CCP and his policies were abandoned. Rise of Liu and Deng and their 'pragmatic' policies.
• **Political:** loss of faith in the CCP when it denied the famine was happening and did not help.
• **Economic:** agricultural production took decades to recover.

Problems with communes

Wheat and rice harvests declined every year from 1958 to 1962. Here are three reasons why:

1 The communes demanded long hours of work, but gave few incentives for hard work. That meant peasants were less productive.

2 Because communes were put together so rapidly, commune administration was often chaotic and driven by Party slogans.

3 Ordering peasants to make steel in backyard furnaces meant that there were fewer people farming, and tools were lost as they were melted down for steel.

Bad weather, 1959–61

The government did not admit there was a famine in China, as this would suggest its policies had gone disastrously wrong. However, it did say bad weather was affecting harvests.

• There were droughts in 1959 and 1960 in important farming areas, such as Sichuan.
• There was heavy rain and flooding in Guangxi in 1959.

However, there was also famine in regions not affected by bad weather.

Lysenkoism and the Four Pests Campaign ended in 1959, but famine continued until 1962.

Government policy

👎 Following Lysenko, communes planted seeds up to ten times closer together than they should be and up to 1.5 metres deep instead of just below the surface. As a result, 90 per cent of the seeds failed to grow.

👎 The Four Pests Campaign (1957) aimed to eliminate four threats to crops: flies, rats, mosquitoes and sparrows, but killed so many sparrows that there was a boom in the crop-eating insects that sparrows usually ate. This then impacted on harvests.

Private farming restored

In 1960, Liu Shaoqi and Deng Xiaoping brought in emergency reforms to tackle the famine. This was 'economic pragmatism'.

✓ Small private farms were allowed; peasants could trade spare food.
✓ Students, soldiers and the unemployed were sent to villages to work on farms.
✓ Communes were reduced in size, priority was given to growing food and hard work was rewarded with pay.

The emergency reforms were successful. Grain production increased by over 60 million tonnes from 1961 to 1966.

Now try this

You will find it helpful to refer to pages 10 and 11, as well as this one, when answering this question.

What reason for the great famine do you think is most convincing? Write a paragraph to explain your answer.

The first Five-Year Plan

In the early 1950s, Chinese communists agreed that China needed to industrialise. There were different ideas about how to do this, and how quickly. In 1953, Mao decided it was time to act.

Reasons for the first Five-Year Plan

In 1953, the CCP began the rapid industrialisation of China. This was a change from Mao's original vision, which was for gradual development of industry – like that in agriculture, 1951–57. Key reasons for this were:

1 The 'success' of Soviet industrialisation, which used five-year plans. In 20 years, Soviet five-year plans had transformed a peasant country into an industrial power.

2 The Korean War (1950–53) made China's leaders worried about foreign invasion. China's military needed to be stronger, which meant modern heavy industry.

3 Maoism and Marxism both taught that socialism and then communism could only be achieved in a fully industrialised society.

Nature of the planned economy

The first Five-Year Plan ran from 1953 to 1957. It was closely modelled on the Soviet model.

- The state took over industries so it could control what they produced. Mao believed this meant China's quite limited resources could be used most efficiently.

- This made China a **planned economy** – rather than industries producing what they thought would make them the most money, government ministries planned what the PRC needed and gave industries targets to meet.

- The state poured investment into industry, especially into the heavy industries: iron, steel, oil and coal.

- Very large new factories were built because large-scale factories would be most efficient.

Industry targets

	1952 production	Planned target
Coal:	68.5m	113 million
Oil:	436m	2012 million
Steel:	1.35m	412 million
Electricity:	7.26b	15.9 billion

1952 production against targets for the end of the first Five-Year Plan (1957). Coal, oil and steel are measured in tonnes, electricity in kWh.

Targets of the first Five-Year Plan

The targets of the first Five-Year Plan focused on rapid development of large-scale heavy industries, for example iron and steel production (90 per cent of state investment went into these heavy industries).

The CCP also planned major improvements to China's **infrastructure** – its roads, railways, bridges and ports. In 1953, there was no bridge across the Yangtze river. The Yangtze divided north and south China. Everything had to be carried over the river by ferry. This was a major obstacle to China's development, so plans were put in place to build a bridge across the river at Wuhan.

Soviet economic aid and technical support

In February 1950, Mao and Stalin agreed the Treaty of Friendship, Alliance and Mutual Assistance. To help China's industrialisation, the USSR committed to providing:

☑ $300 million: though this was a loan with high interest rates. It only made up 3 per cent of investment in the Five-Year Plan.

☑ 156 factories: though, by 1957, less than half of these had been built.

☑ 11000 experts to help run the new factories.

☑ Education for 28000 Chinese technicians.

☑ Detailed plans for factories and machineries.

Now try this

Write a paragraph to explain why the Wuhan bridge was an important part of the first Five-Year Plan.

Plan successes and failures

The first Five-Year Plan was extremely successful. However, it did not meet all its targets and it led to some areas of China becoming more industrialised than others.

Successes of the first Five-Year Plan

👍 The government had set a target of 14.7 per cent growth in industry per year. In fact, industry grew at around 16 per cent per year during 1953–57.

👍 Heavy industrial production tripled in size over the period 1953–57.

👍 Coal, steel and electricity production all exceeded targets: coal = 115 per cent of target; steel = 130 per cent of target; electricity = 122 per cent of target.

👍 Standards of living in the cities improved. Wages increased by nearly 40 per cent.

👍 Urbanisation: the number of people living in cities increased by four million. Urbanised countries have strong economies because there are more people to buy things. This generates more money for manufacturing.

👍 Infrastructure (transport) improved. 6000 km of railway lines were built, connecting China's major cities. The Wuhan bridge across the Yangtze was completed in 1957.

👍 Private industry was abolished, making China more socialist. The last private factories were nationalised in 1956.

Failures of the first Five-Year Plan

👎 The target for oil production was not met – production increased, but only to 73 per cent of the target. As a result, China still had to import most of its oil, which was very expensive.

👎 90 per cent of investment went into heavy industry. Light industry (consumer products) only grew slowly. This was something the second Five-Year Plan tried to focus on.

👎 Pouring investment into industrialisation meant putting off pay rises for workers. This was unpopular and it contributed to the strikes of 1956.

👎 Planning a whole economy was very complex and inefficient. Often a factory had to stop production because the raw materials it needed had failed to arrive.

👎 Soviet aid was problematic. China had to pay high interest payments for loans and send gold to the USSR as security for the loan. It also had to pay for Soviet experts. Expert advice also included Lysenkoism.

For more on the strikes, see page 7.
For more on Lysenkoism, see page 11.

The successes of the first Five-Year Plan were very important for Mao's leadership. They convinced the CCP and the Chinese people that Mao knew exactly how to make China a powerful, modern, socialist country.

Mao was confident that Chinese people now believed in communism. This confidence was important in launching the Hundred Flowers campaign.

For more on the Hundred Flowers campaign, see page 7.

Impact on Mao's leadership

Mao believed central planning was making the CCP too bureaucratic. As a result, he was determined to find ways to involve the 'revolutionary spirit' of the Chinese people.

A third consequence of the success of the first Five-Year Plan was Mao's feeling that China could achieve anything. He made the second Five-Year Plan radical and **utopian** (based on an ideal world).

One propaganda image released to support Mao's leadership was entitled 'Fight for the Overall Completion of the Five-Year Plan Ahead of Time and Exceeding Target Numbers'.

Now try this

Chinese peasants could spend very little on manufactured products. They made most of the things they needed (such as clothes and shoes) themselves. Write a short paragraph to: a) describe how this changed as more people went to live and work in China's cities, and b) explain the effect this had on the economy of the People's Republic of China.

The Great Leap Forward

The second Five-Year Plan was named the Great Leap Forward. Its aims were far more ambitious than the first Five-Year Plan and it was far more radical in its methods. It had disastrous results.

Making China a global power: 'leaping' forward to overtake Western powers like the UK

Cuts in Soviet aid, 1958–62

Mao's faith in mass mobilisation of 'peasant power'

Mao's reasons for the Great Leap Forward

Mao's ideological objections to Soviet-style central planning

Developing agriculture and industry together

China's uneven economic development

Nature of the Great Leap Forward

The second Five-Year Plan was for 1958–62.

- Rather than Soviet-style heavy industry, small-scale production would be prioritised, for example the backyard blast furnaces to produce steel.
- Rather than relying on Soviet-style central planning, mass mobilisation would connect China's economic development to the revolutionary spirit of the Chinese people.
- Industrialisation would take place in each commune, rather than in towns and cities.

Mao turned to China's long history of small-scale rural industry when the USSR cut aid to China between 1958 and 1962. This approach did not need Soviet experts or loans.

Mao wanted to keep the Party connected to peasant power, not to foreign ideas.

The first Five-Year Plan had produced uneven economic development. Mao wanted development to be spread out equally.

The Great Leap Forward was an important cause of the great famine (1958–62). See pages 11–12 for more on why this was the case.

Successes of the Great Leap Forward

- 👍 The communes took up the new policy enthusiastically. Peasants melted down metal tools and equipment, eager to make new, improved steel versions.
- 👍 By the end of 1958, almost 50 per cent of China's steel was produced by small-scale rural factories, based in the communes.
- 👍 The second Five-Year Plan invested in irrigation: providing water to drier farmland so more crops could be grown. The amount of irrigated farmland doubled in 1958.
- 👍 Mao wanted to move away from the Soviet model and combine his idealogy with a Chinese approach.

Targets were set high and officials were put under huge pressure to achieve them. Since failure was not an option, officials forged their reports. This meant problems were not fixed.

Failures of the Great Leap Forward

- 👎 China's industrial output fell by 50 per cent. Output fell by 55 per cent for heavy industry and by 30 per cent for light industry.
- 👎 Steel produced in backyard furnaces was of such poor quality that it could not be used.
- 👎 The pressure to achieve targets meant that production was rushed and products often failed to work.
- 👎 There was economic chaos. The government closed 25 000 state enterprises. New projects were cancelled, and 45 per cent of industrial workers lost their jobs.
- 👎 The failures of the Great Leap Forward were not reported. Instead, officials pretended that everything was going well.

Because peasants had melted down everything metal, and burned everything wooden, to make steel, communes were left without essential tools and equipment.

Now try this

'The main reasons for the Great Leap Forward were ideological – Mao's vision for China.' Give **one** point that supports this interpretation and **one** that counters (goes against) it.

Economic reform

Mao used the Lushan Conference of 1959 to persecute anyone criticising the Great Leap Forward. However, by the end of 1959, Mao realised his policy had failed and allowed others to lead reforms.

The Lushan Conference, 1959

- Peng Dehuai, a military hero, had reported problems with the Great Leap Forward to Mao before the Lushan conference.

- Mao responded by publicly humiliating Peng at the conference and forced him to resign. The conference showed everyone that Mao would not tolerate any criticism.

- The conference led to the 'Anti-Right Opportunist Campaign': this persecuted anyone criticising the Great Leap Forward.

- Mao also promoted a 'second Leap': pushing up production targets still higher.

- As a result, the CCP continued to lie about the terrible economic consequences of the Great Leap Forward, and the start of the great famine. This meant nothing was done to try to reduce the damage.

Economic reforms from 1960

In 1960, pragmatists took control of the CCP's economic policy, led by Deng Xiaoping and Liu Shaoqi.

- Their policies abandoned the Great Leap Forward. For example, in agriculture, private farming was restored. This was less socialist than communes.

- The reforms brought back experts. Experts designed a food rationing system and developed a new variety of rice that increased food supplies. Experts were put in charge of factories.

- Pay was changed so that hard work was rewarded. Discipline was made tougher in factories and farms. This increased production and meant more food supplies.

- Small-scale factories were closed so that resources could be used more efficiently. Backyard furnaces were phased out.

- A 'return to the village' campaign encouraged workers from closed factories to go back to farming, to help improve China's food supply.

- Targets were lowered. This made targets more achievable and reduced the need to forge false statistics.

Reasons for failure

- Mao's faith in the peasants over experts: peasants had no experience in making steel and were not trained to do it.

- Mao's faith in mass mobilisation: 90 million peasants took up the policy, but they lacked the expertise to make it succeed.

- Mao's quarrel with the USSR: Mao disliked Khrushchev's criticisms of Stalin. Once China and the USSR had split, Soviet funding was cut off and Soviet experts left China.

- Targets were set high, but there was no support for how to meet those targets.

- Fear: no one dared to report failures to meet the targets or criticise the policy.

Consequences of failure

- ☑ Mao's loss of authority allowed Liu and Deng to take control of the economy and introduce reforms. Mao withdrew from government.

- ☑ People wanted effective policies to end the famine and raise wages. People lost faith in utopian propaganda.

- ☑ Some historians estimate up to 40 million died due to officials' fear of purges and Mao's refusal to accept criticism.

- ☑ The CCP faced growing lawlessness in famine-struck areas, especially Sichuan and Tibet. Bandits had to be controlled.

Economic recovery to 1965

1. By the end of 1962, the economy was starting to recover.

2. From 1962 to 1965, industry grew at 11 per cent each year.

3. Farming began to recover. Grain production increased by over 60 million tonnes between 1961 and 1966.

4. Urban workers had higher standards of living than peasants. Also, a few peasants became richer while most remained poor. This was not socialism.

Now try this

Explain **three** consequences of the failure of the Great Leap Forward.

The Cultural Revolution

Mao's authority was weakened after the Great Leap Forward. The CCP followed the approach of Liu and Deng, which Mao opposed. The Cultural Revolution helped Mao remove rivals and rival ideas.

Mao's position in government 1960–65

Mao's authority was weakened by the failure of the Great Leap Forward.

- Mao had retreated from an active role in day-to-day government. Liu Shaoqi became president of China, as Mao gave up the presidency. (Mao continued to be chairman of the CCP.)

- The economic policies of Liu Shaoqi and Deng Xiaoping had been successful in ending the great famine. By 1962, the economy was growing again. Senior CCP officials trusted Liu and Deng's economic leadership more than Mao's.

- Between 1962 and 1964, Mao tried to launch five new initiatives, including one to reduce the growth of private farming. Liu and Deng stopped them.

Mao's criticisms of Liu and Deng

Mao opposed what he saw as the **capitalist road** to development that Liu and Deng were following. Instead of the socialist road, which meant peasants and workers benefiting most, Mao said 'capitalist roaders' were making experts and bureaucrats powerful and rich, while the workers and peasants were ignored. Mao also criticised Liu and Deng's policies as **revisionist**: going back on socialist policies and re-introducing capitalist elements. For example:

- Re-introducing private farming and allowing communes to break up.

- Putting experts in charge of factories and planning, instead of letting the workers run the factories themselves.

- Making the CCP bureaucracy more powerful than peasants and workers.

Re-establishing dominance

In the early 1960s, Mao tried to get back control of the CCP. His key allies (supporters) were Lin Biao, defence minister and head of the People's Liberation Army, and Mao's wife, Jiang Qing.

- In 1963, Mao launched the **Socialist Education Movement**, which included plans to remove capitalist elements from the CCP. This would have damaged Liu and Deng.

- Liu and Deng stopped this challenge by putting the CCP in charge of the campaign, not the people. Mao saw that many in the Party did not want his changes.

- In 1965, Mao began a campaign against capitalist culture. Liu and Deng again were able to control the committee organising the campaign.

- The Cultural Revolution began in May 1966. It was supported by Liu and Deng. But, this time, Mao and his allies were better prepared. Liu and Deng were unable to control the new campaign.

Purification of communism: reasons

Mao's campaigns in the 1960s were designed to purge the CCP of capitalist roaders and revisionists, and preserve the spirit of the revolution.

- Instead of elites – Party bureaucrats and industrial experts – Maoism said that everyone in China should be equal.

- Instead of deciding on policies based on whether they were pragmatic (practical), policies should be ideologically correct first. For example, if a policy made some people poorer than others, it could not be correct even if it appeared to have many practical benefits.

- China could achieve anything through the mass mobilisation of its people, as long as the CCP stayed connected to the revolutionary spirit of the people.

- It was the duty of the CCP to organise and lead the people towards communism. This included even leading the people to identify and destroy anything that got in the way of communism.

Now try this

Identify **three** ways in which Mao thought Liu and Deng were taking China on a 'capitalist road'.

Purification of communism

Mao's call for communism to be **purified** (cleansed of capitalist elements) led to the launch of the Cultural Revolution in May 1966. The 'purification of communism' had several key features.

The Socialist Education Movement, 1963

This was Mao's campaign to combat capitalist elements. It began with the launch of Mao's **Ten Points** in January 1963. These strongly criticised revisionism in agriculture.

- Lin Biao introduced a simple version of Mao's ideology, the '**Little Red Book**'. As well as training how to fight, the 'Little Red Book' was used to train soldiers how to think. A campaign to 'learn from the PLA' was part of the Socialist Education Movement.

- Instead of going to school full time, students would spend part of their day working in communes. This combatted education reforms in 1960 that allowed CCP bureaucrats to get their children into better schools.

- Mao said 'experts' and intellectuals should be **re-educated** by working as manual labourers in industry and as peasants in communes.

The Twenty-Three Articles, 1965

- The struggle for control of the CCP meant that Mao's socialist education campaigns had sometimes been controlled and toned down by the moderates Liu and Deng.

- Mao's Twenty-Three Articles stated that the main obstacle to the Socialist Education Movement was enemies within the CCP.

- Mao and his allies called for a purge of corrupt officials within the CCP. They said this purge should be led by groups of peasants and workers.

- Although he didn't challenge Mao directly, Liu Shaoqi blocked this proposal. His concern was that any large-scale attack on China's government would plunge China's economy back into chaos.

Mao used the Twenty-Three Articles to remove his rivals for power. He blamed revisionists within the Party for the re-introduction of capitalist elements into China.

Criticism of the play *Hai Rui dismissed from office* (1965)

The Central Cultural Revolution Group (1966)

The purification of communism: key features

The Twenty-Three Articles (1965)

The Socialist Education Movement (1963)

Make sure you know how each key feature of the purification was linked to Mao's ideology.

Hai Rui dismissed from office

In 1965, Mao began a campaign against capitalist culture in the PRC. This started with criticism of a play written by writer Wu Han called *Hai Rui dismissed from office*.

- ✓ The play, about a 16th-century official who criticised an emperor, was seen as an attack on Mao.

- ✓ Mao's allies said that *Hai Rui* stood for Peng Dehuai, who was dismissed after criticising Mao's Great Leap Forward.

- ✓ The CCP set up a committee – the Five Man Group – to check if a cultural purge was needed. The committee, led by an ally of Liu and Deng, decided that the play was not political. Mao and his allies were outraged and replaced the committee with the new Central Cultural Revolution Group.

The Central Cultural Revolution Group

- ✓ Set up by Mao in May 1966 to lead a culture purge.

- ✓ Led by Jiang Qing, it took control of the CCP's propaganda department.

- ✓ Used propaganda to inspire young people to join 'the Red Guards' to purge the CCP of 'capitalist roaders'.

Now try this

Write a paragraph to explain why Mao set up the Central Cultural Revolution Group.

Student rebellion

In May 1966, the Politburo agreed to launch a Cultural Revolution. By calling on young people to attack his revisionist opponents, Mao created a student rebellion that the CCP could not control.

Mao's hold on young people

Mao appealed to young people to reject CCP 'capitalist roaders'.

- The CCP's education reforms had made it easier for elite CCP officials to get their children into top schools and universities. Other young people resented this.

- In January 1966, the CCP began to distribute copies of the 'Little Red Book' to students. Mao praised young people in this and said that China's future belonged to them.

- Students liked Mao's radical, utopian ideas more than the practical policies of Liu and Deng. Mao's ideas gave young people an exciting, revolutionary role in society.

The Red Guards

The Red Guards were groups of students from universities and schools in cities and towns.

- The first Red Guard group was formed in a middle school in Beijing in 1966. The students were angry about the play *Hai Rui dismissed from office*. They called themselves 'Chairman Mao's Red Guards'.

- Each Red Guard group was organised like an army battalion. Red Guards dressed in a military way and wore red armbands.

- Red Guards were inspired by the PLA and its commitment to revolutionary socialism.

- The Red Guards aimed to fight against capitalist roaders in the CCP and protect Mao and '**Mao Zedong Thought**'.

The mass rallies of 1966

In August 1966, Mao addressed a mass rally of a million Red Guards in Tiananmen Square in Beijing. There were eight mass rallies in total in 1966, attended by around 12 million Guards.

Mao's message was to 'bombard the headquarters'. He criticised the attempts by the CCP to defend itself from the Red Guards. He wanted the Red Guards to pressurise the CCP and force his rivals out.

Reasons why students supported radical change

- Inspiration from *Quotations from Chairman Mao Tse-tung*: the 'Little Red Book'
- Resentment about educational reforms
- Dislike of strict, traditional teachers, who were often arrogant and intimidating
- Idealism – belief in revolutionary socialism
- Respect for Mao as a revolutionary leader
- Poverty, fear of becoming a wealthy target, and peer pressure

Attacks on universities

- In May 1966, Beijing University students protested against their lecturers. In June, these protests turned into physical attacks.

- The students were angry that the lecturers set themselves up as intellectual experts.

- Liu Shaoqi ordered rival Red Guard student groups to be formed, which supported the CCP. Their role was to defend CCP officials from attack by Mao-supporting Red Guards.

- Mao ordered these rival groups to be shut down. In August 1966, in his 16 Articles document, he made the Red Guards free to overthrow 'capitalist roaders' wherever they found them.

Jiang Qing's attack on the CCP

Jiang Qing was the deputy director of the Central Cultural Revolution Group and Mao's wife. She used her control over the CCP's propaganda ministry to encourage Red Guards to attack CCP officials who were suspected 'capitalist roaders'.

Liu Shaoqi and Deng Xiaoping were named as the leaders of the capitalist roaders. Liu was the president of the PRC, China's third most important leader after Mao and Zhou Enlai (the premier). By the end of 1968, Liu was purged.

Now try this

Explain why students supported the Cultural Revolution. Give **three** reasons in your answer.

Red Terror

As Red Guard violence spread throughout China, government began to break down as **anarchy** (chaos) and terror spread.

The 'four olds'

The 'four olds' campaign was launched by Lin Biao at a mass rally in August 1966. The 'four olds' were parts of Chinese culture that had helped to oppress and exploit poor people.

Old ideas   Old customs

The 'four olds'

Old habits   Old culture

The Central Cultural Revolution Group told Red Guard groups across China to attack the 'four olds' wherever they found them. People who read old or foreign books, sung traditional or foreign songs or dedicated themselves to religion were targeted. Many Red Guard groups also used terror to attack authority figures wherever they found them.

Cultural destruction

- Red Guards attacked museums and destroyed old books and artworks. They also attacked religious shrines and temples.

- These attacks even included raiding the tombs of ancient Chinese emperors and mistreating the human remains.

- Red Guards broke into people's homes and destroyed old books, older styles of furniture and religious items. Hundreds of thousands of people lost their possessions and homes.

- Red Guard attacks included attacks on people's hairstyles and clothing, especially if they were seen as Western styles.

- Red Guards replaced old paintings with pictures of Mao. They renamed streets with revolutionary slogans, and even renamed themselves with revolutionary names.

Red Terror: attacks on people

Red Guard attacks on culture quickly turned into attacks on people. Mao encouraged this and the police were forbidden from stopping it.

- Red Guards, dressed in uniforms and carrying 'Little Red Books', patrolled China's towns and cities, targeting intellectuals, bureaucrats and wealthy people.

- People, especially intellectuals, were forced to confess to crimes and were publicly humiliated. Top CCP leaders – accused of being capitalist roaders opposed to Mao Zedong Thought – were also verbally and physically attacked, including Liu, Deng and Peng Dehuai.

- The Red Guards often forced intellectuals and Party officials to do menial jobs, such as sweeping and cleaning toilets.

- Beatings and torture were common. Many people who were targeted for public humiliation committed suicide.

- Several hundred thousand people were beaten to death by the Red Guards. The police did nothing to stop these murders, so the Red Guards continued their violent attacks.

Government breakdown: anarchy

- By the start of 1967, Red Guards were overthrowing the old CCP authorities in towns and cities across China. Even some of the provinces had their Party government purged by the Red Guards.

- Red Guards took over government roles themselves, but different Red Guard groups then fought each other for control. The result was chaos, which meant no government at all – anarchy.

- There was conflict in the countryside between Red Guards who wanted to break up private farming and re-form communes, and peasants who wanted to keep their land.

- Red Guards also fought with industrial workers who did not want to get rid of their managers in case it meant the workers did not get paid their production bonuses.

- All this conflict and chaos meant that China's economic production was badly disrupted.

'Red Terror' is the use of extreme violence to achieve socialist revolutionary aims.

Think about why Peng and other senior CCP officials were out of favour with Mao. You might find pages 16 and 17 helpful.

Now try this

Write a paragraph to explain why Red Guard groups attacked senior CCP officials, such as Peng Dehuai.

Political effects

Mao's Cultural Revolution succeeded in getting rid of his rivals through purges of the CCP. Mao was then able to become China's leader again without anyone to oppose his decisions.

The purging of the CCP

Mao and his allies said that people who wanted to make China capitalist again had secretly worked their way into the CCP. Therefore, the CCP must be purged of anyone suspected of being a revisionist and capitalist roader.

- 28 000 CCP officials were arrested. Hundreds of thousands of lower-level CCP officials were dismissed from their jobs.
- There was a mass purge of senior leaders of the Party; 70 per cent of senior Party members were sent to labour camps for re-education.
- Re-education was often at **May 7th Cadre Schools**. It involved intensive self-criticism and manual labour in large farms or camps. Purged Party members were taught how to serve the people.
- Party officials warned that the purges were destroying the CCP. These 'counter-revolutionaries' were purged as well.

The purging of Liu and Deng

Mao undermined Liu and Deng in a series of steps, ending in their purge from the CCP.

1. Mao said that Liu was China's Khrushchev. Mao said Khrushchev was leading the USSR down a capitalist road.
2. Liu and Deng were forced to make public confessions of their political mistakes at a Party conference in October 1966.
3. In February 1967, Liu and Deng were publicly called counter-revolutionaries.
4. In summer 1967, Liu was put under arrest in his home. In October, he was expelled from the CCP as a traitor.
5. Deng was arrested and sent to a rural tractor factory for re-education and hard labour.
6. Liu was starved, beaten and tortured while under house arrest. He was not allowed medical treatment and died in 1969.

Political chaos

Red Guards led the purging of the CCP. The purges led to many towns and cities being left with no government: even whole provinces.

⬇

Some Red Guard groups set up their own governments. One example is the **Shanghai Commune** (January 1967). This replaced the CCP with an elected city government. The slogan of the commune was 'Do away with all heads' – no more leaders. This showed the Red Guards had not understood Mao's aims.

⬇

Mao condemned this slogan. He did not want other Red Guards to start campaigning for this kind of government as it went against his aim to be a leader that nobody challenged. Mao encouraged the PLA to take control.

Mao set off the Cultural Revolution and encouraged the violent destruction of hundreds of thousands of lives. Only when Red Guards began to challenge his position did he use the PLA to bring the chaos under control.

The rise and fall of Lin Biao

- Lin Biao was a key ally for Mao in building up to and launching the Cultural Revolution.
- In 1966, Mao had named him as his successor.
- In 1969, Lin Biao was very powerful, making the main speech at the National Party Conference.
- Lin Biao was the leader of the PLA from September 1959. The PLA had taken control over the revolutionary committees that ran cities and provinces.
- Zhou Enlai warned that the purges had made the CCP so weak that Lin Biao could use the PLA to take control of China. Mao listened.
- Mao and Zhou began to rebuild the CCP, bringing back purged officials. As the CCP took back control, the importance of the PLA in governing China was reduced. This made Lin Biao less important.
- In 1971, Lin Biao was accused of being in a mysterious plot to assassinate Mao. It was said he had then died attempting to flee to the USSR in an aeroplane that had crashed.

Now try this

Write a paragraph to explain why the Shanghai Commune was a threat to Mao.

Social and economic effects

The Cultural Revolution had a major impact on Chinese society, especially on education. Its economic impacts were also very disruptive, especially for city industries.

Social effects: social disruption

1 Death and misery: as many as 400000 people died from Red Guard attacks. Millions were tortured, imprisoned or sent for re-education and hard labour.

2 Guilt: some Red Guards questioned whether they had been right to persecute their teachers. This guilt lasted decades.

3 Disruption to education: most universities were closed until 1972, and thousands of university teachers were sent for re-education. Many Red Guards also were sent to work in the countryside. Millions of students did not complete their studies and many schools closed as a result.

4 Disruption to work: many factories were closed and people became unemployed.

Social: Education reforms

Social: Disruption – closing schools, universities, factories

Economic: Move to countryside

Social and economic effects of the Cultural Revolution

Economic: Declining production

Economic: Impact on farming

Economic: Changes in industry

Social effects: impact on education

Mao introduced education reforms during and after the Cultural Revolution.

- More funding was given to poor students in rural areas. Better-off students in city areas got less funding. This made it easier for poorer students to get a good education.

- There were 15 times as many rural primary schools in 1976 compared with 1965. This happened because the government made schooling compulsory for five years. As a result, more children in poorer areas were able to go to school.

- Before 1972, universities had decided which students should have places by looking at their scores in tests. After 1972, this was changed. Now universities had to consider references about the student. This helped students from poorer areas get into university as these students often did less well in the tests.

As a result of education reforms, China's literacy rate increased to 65 per cent by 1982.

Economic effects: changes in industry

- Millions of technicians, experts and managers were persecuted in the Cultural Revolution and killed, imprisoned or exiled to labour camps or remote rural communes.

- China's industries were in choas. There was a major decline in industrial output. In 1967, industrial production dropped by 13 per cent.

- Reforms in 1969 made conditions more equal for all workers. Bonuses or overtime payments were stopped. Managers had to spend one-third of their time doing factory work rather than administration.

- But these changes did not last long. In 1972, the CCP needed to promote economic growth. Managers were paid more again.

Economic effects: impact on farming

- Around two-thirds of privately farmed land was returned to communes in 1966.

- Private trade in farm products was banned. Communes grew crops for the state.

- The move to the countryside meant more small industry moved to rural areas, for example workshops that repaired farm machinery and small fertiliser factories.

Now try this

Why did China's literacy rate increase to 65 per cent by 1982? Give **two** reasons.

Winding down

Mao used different approaches to break up the Red Guards at the end of the Cultural Revolution. He worked with Zhou Enlai to rebuild the Chinese Communist Party.

The end of the Red Guards

By 1967, radical Red Guard groups wanted an end to central Party control. This challenged Mao's dictatorship. He used different strategies to **demobilise** (break up) the Red Guards.

1 In spring 1968, Mao ordered the Red Guards to demobilise. The majority did not.

2 In August 1968, Mao used the PLA to break up Red Guard groups by force. This was after violence at Beijing University.

3 From December 1968, the 'Up to the mountains, down to the villages' campaign was introduced.

Mao used the PLA to crush the Red Guards. This increased the power of the PLA in China. As a result, Mao then needed to rebuild the power of the CCP.

Increased influence of Zhou Enlai

With Liu and Deng purged, Mao turned to Zhou Enlai to help rebuild the CCP. Zhou was an old ally of Mao and an excellent administrator.

- After Lin Biao died in 1971, Zhou began to bring back purged CCP officials into government.

- In 1972–73, Zhou **reinstated** 700 senior CCP officials and 150 senior military leaders – he allowed them to return to their old roles.

- This helped to get the government back to running efficiently again because these were experienced officials who knew what to do.

Although Zhou Enlai was not a supporter of the Cultural Revolution, he avoided being purged himself. He was very careful not to criticise Mao and was a very valuable Party official. However, his adopted daughter was killed by Red Guards in the Cultural Revolution.

'Up to the mountains and down to the villages'

In this campaign, Mao ordered the PLA to transport millions of young people to the countryside for re-education in order to prevent further chaos in the cities. This also aimed to decrease urban unemployment caused by the Cultural Revolution.

Mao claimed Red Guard violence showed that students needed to learn discipline.

More than 17 million young people were moved out of the cities in this way between 1968 and 1976. Most did not find a way to return to their cities again.

The return of Deng Xiaoping

- Zhou had argued that Liu and Deng should be allowed to return to the CCP soon after they were purged. But Mao and Lin Biao refused to allow this.

- After Lin Biao died, Zhou criticised him and the PLA for persecuting CCP members. Deng was allowed to re-join the CCP in March 1973. (Liu Shaoqi had died in 1969.)

- By August 1973, Deng had got back many of his old powers. For example, he was again a member of the Politburo.

- Deng's return had important consequences. Both Zhou and Mao were old and ill. By the end of 1975, Deng was China's main leader.

The restoration of order

| **1968**: PLA ordered to break up Red Guards; 'Up to the mountains and down to the villages' campaign begins | **1971**: Death of Lin Biao; Zhou Enlai begins reinstating officials | **1973**: Deng Xiaoping returns to government | **1975**: Deng appointed to senior Party roles | **1976**: Death of Zhou (January); Death of Mao (September) |

Now try this

Think about the influence of Zhou and why Deng's experience of government might be useful.

In a short paragraph, explain why Mao agreed Deng could return to the CCP. Give **at least one** reason.

The Gang of Four

As Zhou Enlai and Mao Zedong reached the end of their lives, there was a power struggle in the CCP. Deng supported Zhou's moderate, practical approach, but the 'Gang of Four' wanted to continue radical policies in a second Cultural Revolution.

Jiang Qing

- Intellectual
- Member of Central Cultural Revolution Group
- Interested in Chinese culture
- Encouraged radicalism in Cultural Revolution
- Mao's wife

Zhang Chunqiao

- Writer
- Member of Central Cultural Revolution Group
- Jiang's ally in Cultural Revolution
- Leader of Shanghai Commune

The 'Gang of Four'

Yao Wenyuan

- Literary critic
- Member of Central Cultural Revolution Group
- Criticised *Hai Rui*, as instructed by Jiang Qing
- Propagandist for Politburo

Wang Hongwen

- Red Guard
- Helped create Shanghai Commune
- 1976, vice-chairman of CCP

Rise and fall of the 'Gang of Four'

1 The 'Gang of Four' all wanted to see radical political and economic change continue in China. They were all important in the Cultural Revolution.

2 As Mao became ill in his last years, the 'Gang of Four' worked hard to build a powerbase in the CCP. They wanted to make sure Mao's radical ideas continued after his death.

3 Their opponents in the CCP were Zhou Enlai and his ally, Deng Xiaoping. Deng's return in 1973 made Zhou stronger. They formed a moderate, practical group in the Party.

4 The 'Gang of Four' were all given important positions in the Politburo by Mao in 1973, which led to faction fighting between them and Zhou. Jiang Qing launched a campaign that tried to link Zhou with Lin Biao. Since his death, Lin Biao was hated as a traitor to China.

5 In January 1976, Zhou Enlai died. He was very popular in China and people wanted to go to public events about him. But the 'Gang of Four' would not allow this. They prohibited **public mourning** for Zhou – in case it encouraged opposition to their plans.

6 The move to prohibit public mourning or tributes to Zhou was extremely unpopular. Thousands of people ignored the ban and went to Tiananmen Square. There were tributes to Zhou, but also protests against the 'Gang of Four'.

7 The 'Gang of Four' responded with a severe crackdown on the 'counter-revolutionaries'. The police violently drove the people away from Tiananmen Square. People protesting against the 'Gang of Four' were executed.

8 The 'Gang of Four' also linked Deng to the protests in Tiananmen Square. Mao, very ill, supported the 'criticise Deng' campaign. In April 1976, Deng was purged for a second time.

9 The 'Gang of Four's' brutal response to the 'Tiananmen Incident' made them even more unpopular. When Mao died in September 1976, the 'Gang of Four' seemed to prepare to take over power by force. They ordered supporters in Shanghai to arm the militias they controlled.

10 Other members of the Politburo joined together with PLA leaders to bring down the 'Gang of Four', before they took over by force. They were arrested in October 1976. They and their supporters were sent to prison. There were public celebrations. Chinese media blamed them for Cultural Revolution terror.

Now try this

Pages 18 and 21 will help you answer this question.

The Central Cultural Revolution Group, *Hai Rui dismissed from office* and the Shanghai Commune were all important in the Cultural Revolution. Write a paragraph to explain how they are all linked to the 'Gang of Four'.

Propaganda and censorship

The CCP had complete control of China's media. They used this to make sure that Chinese people experienced positive messages about communism and did not experience alternative views.

Censorship

Censorship means removing 'undesirable' ideas from the media. The CCP used censorship of books, films, music and the arts.

- All book publishing was controlled through the People's Publishing House. The Publications Administration Bureau banned 6766 of the 8000 books published in China pre-1949. During the Cultural Revolution, only books written by Mao were published. Books with 'old ideas' were destroyed.

- The Film Bureau censored Western films, removing or over-dubbing parts judged as counter-revolutionary.

- Only art and music that served communism was tolerated. The 1960 Congress of Artists controlled artistic production.

Propaganda and agit-prop

Propaganda is false or one-sided information used by a government or political group to make people agree with them. Thousands of people worked as propagandists for the CCP, using newspapers (*The People's Daily*), radio (Central People's Broadcasting), film and books to deliver their messages. Radio was used widely to reach people unable to read.

One important type of propaganda was **agit-prop**: agitation propaganda, which aims to mobilise people to do something.

It used every type of media: posters, newspapers, school lessons, songs. Agit-prop plays toured round China's countryside, using simple plots to teach the audience to abandon old ideas and take up new, socialist methods.

The 'cult of Mao'

Propaganda created an image of Mao as a god-like leader whose ideas were never wrong and who lived only to care for the Chinese people.

- The 'Little Red Book' was viewed almost like a sacred text. People would read the book for guidance on problems in their lives. Studying and understanding Mao's writings were essential for any Party member.

- The 'cult of Mao' grew rapidly during the Cultural Revolution, 1965–68. Red Guards worshipped Mao and vowed to protect Mao Zedong Thought against all opponents.

- The 'cult of Mao' was important because it gave Mao power to unleash social forces, as seen with young people – the Red Guards.

战无不胜的毛泽东思想万岁！
LONG LIVE THE INVINCIBLE THOUGHT OF MAO TSE-TUNG!

Poster sign outside a Chinese hotel

Propaganda: campaigns

Propaganda was very important in the CCP's many campaigns. Three examples are:

1. The 1950 **Resist America, Aid Korea** campaign: propaganda convinced two million volunteers to fight for North Korea and encouraged people to support the war effort. Propaganda explained the war as China's fight against capitalist enemies.

2. The 1955 **campaign against Hu Feng**: Hu Feng, a communist, criticised Mao's ideas on culture in a report to the CCP. Propaganda portrayed Hu as a GMD agent and encouraged people to search out supporters of Hu. Hu's trial and sentence to a labour camp were also used to warn people about counter-revolutionaries.

3. The 1963 **cult of Lei Feng**: Lei Feng was a PLA soldier who died in 1962. Films about Lei Feng celebrated his many good deeds and showed him as constantly reading Mao's writing and expressing his love for Mao. It is likely that all this was made up, but the campaign was very successful.

Now try this

During 1950 and 1951, Red Drama Groups toured China's countryside putting on plays in which peasants seized land from wicked landlords. Explain why this is an example of agit-prop.

Thought control

Marxist theory states that the working class struggles to be free of the capitalist class that exploits it. Mao's ideology taught that ideas were part of this struggle, too. Communist ideas were in a struggle with capitalist ideas. **Thought control** aimed to help communist ideas win this struggle.

Self-criticism

- Maoism viewed capitalist ideas as a poison or disease that could be removed from a person through self-criticism.
- Self-criticism meant examining your actions and searching out mistakes you had made.
- People were encouraged to criticise themselves for being selfish, because selfishness was capitalist while socialists always worked for the benefit of others.

An example is Zhou Enlai's 1951 campaign against intellectuals. As part of this, 3000 university teachers were required to carry out public self-criticism, confess their capitalist views and then engage in study sessions about Marxism.

Struggle meetings

- Struggle meetings involved crowds of people humiliating and hurting victims to make them confess to capitalist crimes or counter-revolutionary thoughts and actions.
- They were called struggle meetings because of the class struggle. Ideologically, they were supposed to be helping the victim because they forced them to confront their wrong thoughts and actions.
- By involving work colleagues or crowds of people, struggle sessions spread thought control ideas out to large numbers of people. No one wanted to be the next victim. People made sure they said the 'right' things.

Re-education through labour

Mao believed that people from capitalist classes naturally had capitalist ideas. That was the reason why people from the 'black categories' were classed as enemies of the people. People didn't choose their ideas and thoughts; they were 'determined' or fixed for them by their class background.

However, some classes naturally developed socialist ideas: the working class and the poorer peasant class. So, if people from a capitalist class were put into a working-class job, the job would naturally teach them correct, socialist ideas.

'Reform Through Labour'

- The 'Reform Through Labour' system (**Laogai** in Mandarin) was a network of thousands of large forced-labour camps set up by Mao in 1957.
- Mao involved Soviet experts in planning and constructing the *Laogai* camps: they were modelled on the USSR's *Gulag* system.
- The *Laogai* system was designed to re-educate and reform people through work for the good of the people of China.
- In practice, the system created huge concentration camps where millions of people were forced to work in horrific conditions.
- The camps were built all over China. Many were located in remote, sparsely populated areas with harsh climates. As a result, it was difficult to escape from them.
- The camps were important to China's economy. Prisoners worked on making consumer goods, building factories, farming and in China's dangerous mines.
- About 25 million people died in *Laogai* camps between 1949 and 1976 because of the terrible working and living conditions.

From Marxism to thought control

Marxist views on class struggle

↓

Mao's view that ideas were part of the class struggle

↓

Thought control

↓   ↓   ↓

| Self-criticism and struggle sessions | Laogai system | Re-education through labour |

Now try this

Write a paragraph to explain the link between the 'Up to the mountains and down to the villages' campaign and thought control.

You will need to use page 23 as well as this one in your answer.

Changes in family life

Mao thought that the traditional Chinese family needed reform because it encouraged oppression of women, and its customs and practices kept Chinese people tied to old beliefs.

Marxist ideology said that the traditional family structure exploited women. Women must be freed from male oppression to become workers for the state.

In the countryside, several generations lived together as extended families. With **industrialisation**, people moved to cities, leaving relatives behind to live in **nuclear** families: parents and children.

Communes   Cultural Revolution

Ideology and cultural reform

Changes in family life

Changes for women and attitudes to women

Urbanisation   Land reform   Collectivisation

Popular attitudes to women

Traditional Chinese families were dominated by men, who had all the power. Under communism, women had more equal rights.

Impact of land reform and collectivisation

- ✓ Land reform gave peasants more land. This meant rising living standards – families had more to eat and could make more money selling food.
- ✓ Collectivisation encouraged peasant families to pool their possessions and land together. Children no longer inherited property from parents and this encouraged young people to move to cities.

The Cultural Revolution and family worship

Traditional Chinese families practised ancestor worship. This involved the family paying respect to dead ancestors at family shrines. It was very important for family identity.

The Cultural Revolution included attacks on Chinese traditions, breaking up shrines and tablets sacred to family ancestors. This made it hard for families to continue ancestor worship because, when sacred items were broken, this also broke the connection to ancestors' spirits.

Changes for women

The Marriage Law (1950) gave women far more rights, including divorce rights. Families changed as women used their right to divorce. In some rural areas, the divorce rate was especially high: young married couples divorced to get out of arranged marriages.

In rural areas, men complained of the 'three fears': not finding a wife, being unable to provide for a wife and being divorced.

The impact of communes

Communes were organised so that family commitments did not interfere with work.

- There were communal canteens so women did not have to spend time away from work making family meals.
- The communes had childcare facilities. This meant mothers did not have to spend time away from work looking after children.
- In some communes, men and women lived separately, even if they were married. The idea was that individuals worked for the benefit of everyone, not just their family.
- These radical changes to family life failed to meet their aims. Instead of being freed to work, mothers ended up having to work **as well as** support family life.
- Because communes were so large, canteens were often miles away from family homes. Time saved not cooking was therefore spent travelling instead.
- Communes did not spend much money on childcare: there were few things for children to do and not much to eat. Illnesses spread quickly. This all meant additional childcare at home.

Now try this

Explain why communes wanted to reduce family commitments, for example by providing childcare, communal canteens and laundry services. In your answer, evaluate how well this worked in practice.

Changes for women

Before 1949, women had a very low **status** in Chinese society. Women were seen as useful only in terms of what they could do for men. Mao's socialism aimed to end all oppression and inequality.

Status of women before 1949

Here are three examples of women's low status in Chinese society before 1949.

- ✓ *San gang* – the 'Three Guiding Principles' from **Confucian philosophy** (ancient Chinese way of thinking) – taught that women had to obey their husbands.
- ✓ Wife selling – husbands could sell their wives if they had an affair or ran away.
- ✓ Foot binding – men considered it beautiful for women to have tiny feet. Girls suffered agonising foot binding as a result.

Before 1949, weddings were often arranged by a female 'matchmaker'. The couple involved did not make the decision themselves. Having more than one wife, or having a wife and several concubines, was common in some areas.

The Marriage Law, 1950

The Marriage Law abolished **feudal** (traditional) marriage laws.

- Forced marriages were made illegal and the right of 'matchmakers' to arrange marriages ended.
- Children being married, men living with concubines or having multiple wives, and dowries all became illegal.
- Women could now own and inherit property in the same way men did. Before, the husband owned everything and his wife had no right to what the family earned.
- Women had equal rights to men in all areas.
- Divorce was legalised and wife-selling was made illegal.
- Abuse and bad treatment of women by men within the family was made illegal.

In some areas, as many as a quarter of young couples got divorced. Of these divorces, 76 per cent were driven by the woman.

Reasons for change under Mao

Mao's beliefs drove change.

- He was influenced early on by Chinese feminism.
- Socialism meant ending all oppression in society, including of women by men.
- China's industrialisation and modernisation depended on women, as well as men, being educated and working.
- Mao believed traditional forms of marriage oppressed women.

Mao had been forced into an arranged marriage and hated it. His mother, who Mao loved deeply, had her feet bound as a girl.

Foot binding became illegal in 1949, but was still practised in remote rural areas. In 1950, Mao ordered that any women found still binding their feet were to be publicly shamed so that this extremely oppressive practice would disappear.

The number of child marriages dropped by 85 per cent between 1949 and 1965.

The PLA gave land to women as well as men during land reform, so women were no longer dependent on men.

Continuing inequalities

- Although more women went to work, they tended to get lower paid jobs than men.
- Even though both men and women were working, women were still expected to do the majority of housework.
- During the Cultural Revolution, Red Guards would punish women who wore feminine clothes or had long hair. Women were expected to dress in a certain style.
- Men dominated the CCP. Fewer than 13 per cent of CCP officials were women between 1949 and 1965.

Now try this

Explain **three** ways in which the status of women (their importance) changed under Mao's leadership.

Changes in education

Education reforms in the 1950s led to big increases in **literacy** levels, but the Cultural Revolution created a 'lost generation' of students who missed out on all or part of their education.

Reasons for changes in education

There were three main reasons why Mao and the CCP reformed education in China:

- ✓ Chinese education was only for the **elite**. In 1949, only 20 per cent of people could read and write, because only the children of richer people went to school.
- ✓ Before 1949, Chinese education was old-fashioned: it was based on the ancient teachings of **Confucius**; girls were rarely educated.
- ✓ Mao wanted people to read to help the CCP spread their message.

Mao and the CCP wanted to end elitism in education. Instead, everyone should have a basic education, to help build economic growth.

Mao opposed intellectuals because their traditional ideas blocked the revolutionary socialism of the peasants and workers.

The success of the 'Little Red Book' as propaganda was based on Chinese soldiers, peasants and workers being literate.

The growth in literacy

- Education reforms in the 1950s created a national network of primary schools. Now millions more children could go to school.
- In 1958, *Pinyin* was introduced, which made written Mandarin easier to learn.
- Literacy drives improved adult literacy with short-term schools and winter schools for workers and peasants.

Literacy rates improved from 20 per cent in 1949 to 50 per cent in 1960. By 1976, they were at 70 per cent!

Significance of *Pinyin*

Pinyin means 'spelled sounds'. There was no single way of writing China's many languages and dialects. The official language of the PRC, Mandarin, was written in a very complicated way – learning it was very difficult. Pinyin was much simpler to learn and was introduced as the standard way to write across China, enabling faster growth in literacy.

Běijīng Shì   北京市

'Beijing' written in Pinyin (left) and Mandarin (right).

The collapse of education after 1966

The Cultural Revolution affected education.

- 👎 During 1966, thousands of middle schools and all universities closed, affecting 130 million students.
- 👎 Thousands of teachers and lecturers were killed or sent for re-education.
- 👎 The 'Up to the mountains and down to the villages' campaign (1968) ended the education of around 100 million young people.
- 👍 From 1969, education was boosted by more rural primary schools and more equal access to learning.

象雷锋那样努力学习

This poster from the Cultural Revolution says: 'Study Hard Follow Lei Feng'.

Now try this

You will need to look at page 25 as well as this page to answer this question.

Study the poster above from the Cultural Revolution. What message does it give about what the CCP wanted education to achieve in the PRC? Explain your answer in a paragraph.

29

Changes in health provision

The CCP wanted to provide **health provision** (such as hospitals and doctors) equally for all Chinese people, but healthcare was very expensive to provide on such a huge scale.

Reasons for changes in health provision

- Before 1949, only a few people, the elite, could afford access to modern healthcare or lived in the big cities – the only place it was provided. Everyone else relied on traditional peasant remedies. Remote rural locations had very little access to healthcare.
- The CCP wanted good healthcare to be provided to everyone across China, including remote rural locations, to ensure a healthy workforce.
- Mao was against experts in Western medicine, which included the government officials running China's health ministry.

Healthcare provision for all

1. As communes were set up in the Great Leap Forward, each commune had a health station – a medical clinic.

2. In 1965, Mao moved doctors and health workers out of cities to carry out hygiene campaigns in China's countryside.

3. State investment in healthcare: by 1965, the government had paid for 100 000 people to train to be fully-qualified doctors. The state had also built more than 800 modern hospitals.

For more on the Great Leap Forward, see page 15.

Significance of barefoot doctors

Commune medics, like most peasants, rarely wore shoes. They became known as '**barefoot doctors**'.

By 1965, there were around 250 000 barefoot doctors. By 1970, there were one million.

Barefoot doctors could provide basic, free medical care in remote villages. They sent more seriously ill people to hospital.

A military doctor training young women to become barefoot doctors.

Peasants often used human waste as manure, risking water-borne diseases like cholera. Barefoot doctors were trained to educate them about hygiene and sanitation (disposing of human waste). This was backed up by campaigns called patriotic health movements.

Barefoot doctors were trained to give vaccination injections, for example against smallpox. This made a big contribution to creating a healthier workforce for the PRC.

Successes of changes in health provision

- 👍 Life expectancy (how long people can expect to live) increased in China from 36 years in 1949 to 66 years in 1976.
- 👍 Infant mortality (the number of babies that die per 1000 births) dropped from 130 per 1000 in 1950 to 60 per 1000 in 1976.
- 👍 By 1976, 85 per cent of rural China's population had access to a doctor.
- 👍 Because barefoot doctors were paid by their commune as a percentage of what the commune made, they were very cheap. The CCP provided basic healthcare for all without taking investment away from industry.

Failures of changes in health provision

- 👎 Limited hospital places – there were only two million hospital beds for a population of 900 million people.
- 👎 In the Cultural Revolution, Mao ordered 'intellectual' doctors in the cities to go and train barefoot doctors. This meant medical research suffered, and city populations had worse medical care.
- 👎 China made huge healthcare improvements under Mao, but it was starting from a very low level. Barefoot doctors only gave basic care, without access to expensive modern Western drugs.

Now try this

List and explain **three** ways in which barefoot doctors improved health provision in China.

Attacks on traditional culture

Mao and the CCP believed that traditional Chinese culture was an obstacle to socialism. They believed it needed to be attacked, purged and replaced by a culture of revolutionary socialism.

Attacks in the countryside

- In the countryside, the CCP attacked culture based on **Confucianism** (the basis of Chinese property laws). This was seen as landlord culture, used to justify the landlords exploiting the peasants.
- In 1950, a 'cultural army' of **Red Drama Groups** began to visit rural areas, especially areas that had been under GMD control.
- Red Drama Groups performed radical plays, operas and ballets that helped explain CCP ideology.
- Red Drama Groups aimed to encourage peasants to take action, for example to seize land from landlords.

The White-haired Girl tells the story of a group of peasants who rebel against a landlord. It was performed by Red Drama Groups and was watched by huge crowds.

Attacks in the towns and cities

- In the towns, the CCP attacked **bourgeois** (capitalist) culture. This was seen as a selfish culture based on getting more possessions and money.
- Theatre directors were targeted for struggle sessions and physical attacks. They were attacked as rightists.
- Culture was reformed so that working class and peasant characters were made heroic. Previously, peasant characters had often been portrayed as stupid or devious.
- The CCP also attacked Western ideas in Chinese culture, especially those that encouraged selfishness and individualism.
- Attacking Western ideas included physical attacks on people wearing Western clothes or makeup, reading Western books or listening to Western music.

The imposition of revolutionary art and culture

Jiang's motives:

- Mao told his wife Jiang Qing to be the 'cultural purifier of the nation': her job was to purge Chinese culture of traditional or Western ideas.
- Jiang had been an actress and knew about theatre.
- She was a radical, strongly motivated by Maoism.
- As a politician, she wanted to build a powerbase and remove opponents.

Jiang's role:

- Jiang was a leader of the Central Cultural Revolution Group, leading the Cultural Revolution.
- She led propaganda campaigns against the 'four olds'.
- She controlled censorship in the Cultural Revolution.
- She commissioned new art to inspire revolutionary ideas and impose revolutionary culture.

A propaganda poster showing Jiang Qing.

Jiang's censorship

Under Jiang, almost all the operas, plays and ballets written before the Cultural Revolution were banned. Jiang was strongly opposed to any traditional or Western cultural influences. Instead, Jiang demanded that the arts should be 'red, bright and shining' – revolutionary.

Re-education of artists

Art that did not inspire and educate the Chinese people about Maoism was suspected of intellectualism, rightism and bourgeois ideas. Artists were sent to rural areas for re-education. Working as peasants would help them connect their art with the goal of serving the people.

Now try this

Don't forget the role of women. You can find out more on page 28.

List **three** reasons to explain why the CCP attacked traditional culture. Give an example for each reason you list.

Attacks on religion

Article 88 of the Chinese constitution of 1954 said that people in China could follow any religion, or none. In practice, the government saw religions as a threat and persecuted religious leaders.

Attacking Buddhism

- When China invaded Tibet in 1950, the CCP banned Tibetan Buddhism to prevent resistance.
- The CCP attacked Buddhist monks in China as lazy people who did no useful work, living off the work of other people.
- During the Korean War (1950–53), persecution of Buddhists increased. Buddhism was important in South Korea at the time.
- During the 'four olds' campaign, Buddhist temples were destroyed; Buddhist monks were killed or sent to *Laogai* camps.

> Buddhism was a major religion in China, and a key part of Tibetan culture, in 1949.

Attacking Confucianism

- The CCP attacked Confucianism because it supported traditional roles in society.
- From the start of the PRC, Confucianism was blamed for the oppression of peasants and women. Confucian thought stressed the need to respect those in authority.
- Confucian temples and shrines were destroyed as part of the 'four olds' campaign.
- After Lin Biao's death, he was criticised as being influenced by Confucianism.

> Confucianism is an ancient Chinese set of morals and philosophy. It was very widespread in Chinese culture in 1949.

Attacking Christianity

- The CCP's Religious Affairs Department ordered Christian missionaries to leave China. By 1953, almost all had left.
- The government took over hospitals, schools and universities that had been set up by Christian missionaries.
- Christians were encouraged to join the Patriotic Three-Self Church, set up and controlled by the CCP. Many Protestant Christians refused and went to secret house-churches instead.
- House-church leaders were arrested. For example, Pastor Samuel Lamb (Lin Xiangao) was sent to a labour camp for 20 years.
- A CCP campaign against the Catholic Church accused Catholics of murdering children.
- The pope did not want Roman Catholics to join the government's Church and threatened to **excommunicate** (exclude) any clerics appointed by the CCP.
- All remaining Catholic Churches were closed down during the Cultural Revolution.

> The CCP saw Christianity as a way for Westerners to control the Chinese people.

Attacking Islam

- Most of China's Muslims lived in the north-west. The CCP thought that this region might try to join neighbouring Muslim countries.
- Muslim schools were closed so that children went to state schools that did not teach anything positive about Islam.
- In the Cultural Revolution, pigs were slaughtered in mosques and imams (priests) were forced to breed pigs and eat pork – all strongly prohibited in Islam.

> Islamic values were a challenge to the CCP.

Attacking ancestor worship

- The CCP attacked ancestor worship as an old way of thinking – an obstacle to socialism.
- Campaigns encouraged people to stop superstitious practices like making offerings.
- Communal living weakened the link between people and their family traditions.

> In 1949, traditions about honouring the dead were widespread in China. These traditions survived: after Mao's death, many felt guided by his spirit.

Now try this

> Think about the CCP's ideas about control and independence, as well as useful work.

Identify **three** reasons why the CCP did not want people in the PRC to follow religions. Give **one** example for each reason.

Exam overview

This page introduces you to the main features and requirements of the Paper 3 Option 32 exam paper.

About Paper 3

Paper 3 is for your modern depth study:

- Mao's China, 1945–76 is a modern depth study and is Option 32.

- It is divided into two sections: Section A and Section B. You must answer **all** questions in **both** sections.

- You will receive two documents: a question paper, which you write on, and a Sources/Interpretations Booklet, which you will need for Section B.

> ⏱ The Paper 3 exam lasts for 1 hour 20 minutes (80 minutes). There are 52 marks in total. You should spend approximately 25 minutes on Section A and 55 minutes on Section B.

> You can see examples of all six questions on pages 35–41, and in the practice questions on pages 42–55.

The questions

The questions for Paper 3 will always follow this pattern:

Section A: Question 1

Give **two** things you can infer from Source A about …   **(4 marks)**

Complete the table.

> Question 1 targets AO3 (analysing, evaluating and using sources to make judgements). Spend about six minutes on this question, which focuses on **inference** and **analysing** sources. Look out for the key term 'infer'.

Section A: Question 2

Explain why …   **(12 marks)**

Two prompts and your own information.

> Question 2 targets both AO1 (showing knowledge and understanding of the topic) and AO2 (explaining and analysing events using historical concepts such as causation, consequences, change, continuity, similarity and difference). Spend approximately 18 minutes on this question.

Section B: Question 3(a)

How useful are Sources B and C for an enquiry into …?   **(8 marks)**

Use the sources and your knowledge of the historical context.

> Question 3(a) also targets AO3. Spend about 12 minutes on this question, which is about **evaluating the usefulness** of contemporary sources.

Section B: Question 3(b)

Study Interpretations 1 and 2 …

What is the main difference between these views?   **(4 marks)**

Use details from both interpretations.

> Questions 3(b) and 3(c) target AO4 (analysing, evaluating and making judgements about interpretations). Spend about six minutes on each of these questions, which are about **suggesting and explaining why** the interpretations differ.

Section B: Question 3(c)

Suggest **one** reason why Interpretations 1 and 2 give different views about …   **(4 marks)**

You can use the sources provided to help explain your answer.

> Question 3(d) also targets AO4. Spend about 30 minutes on this question, which is about **evaluating** an interpretation. Up to 4 marks are available for **spelling, punctuation and grammar (SPaG) and use of specialist terminology.**

Section B: Question 3(d)

How far do you agree with Interpretation 1/2 about …? **(16 marks + 4 marks for SPaG and use of specialist terminology)**

Use both interpretations and your knowledge of the historical context.

Sources and interpretations

This exam asks you to analyse and evaluate both sources and interpretations, and you need different skills for each.

Questions 1 and 3(a)

Here you will be asked to look at sources. These sources could be propaganda posters, accounts from people at that time, photographs, or any written or visual source that is **from the period**. As the sources are generated from that time, it is helpful to think about the nature of the source, its origin, who produced it, and the purpose for which it was produced.

Questions 3(b), (c) and (d)

Here you will be asked to read interpretations of a particular enquiry or event from two different historians. Unlike analysing sources, interpretations are written **after the time period or event**. They are often written by historians or commentators who express their views and opinions about historical people, events and changes. As they are people's views and judgements based on evidence, there can be differences, and sometimes clear disagreements, about what people think.

Content: what information can you get directly from the source and its caption? It is important to spend time reading and studying sources before you read the exam questions.

Nature: what type of source is it – a diary entry, newspaper article, cartoon? This will help you assess its reliability, usefulness and purpose.

Origin: the caption should tell you who produced the source and when. The origin will help you assess its reliability, usefulness and purpose.

Purpose: the reason a source was created could be one of the questions by itself, but this will also help you to assess its reliability and usefulness.

> **Hints and tips for examining sources**

Bias: a source is still useful even if you think it is biased – it can be good for assessing people's opinions of an event, for example.

Language: in written sources, the author's language should give you clues about whether they are biased or even unreliable. Using appropriate examples by quoting directly from the source will help you gain better marks. Language can also tell you about the purpose of a source.

Selection: what has the author/artist chosen to include? What have they chosen to leave out? It's important to consider both of these when you are thinking about the reliability, usefulness and purpose of a source.

Hints and tips for analysing and evaluating interpretations

How complete?	How objective?	What is the chosen emphasis?
The two interpretations can be different because they are concerned with finding out about different aspects of the enquiry and may cover different ground. Sometimes historians set out to look at one aspect specifically, whereas others may want to look at related issues in a broader sense.	Historians can hold different views because they come from a particular school of thought. Therefore, their questions and answers are shaped by their wider views of society and how it works and has worked in the past. This can have an important impact on the judgements and opinions they hold about historical matters.	Sometimes, historians use the same sources but reach different views because they place a different level of importance on the same evidence. They may have access to the same material sources as each other, but will draw different conclusions about the significance of that evidence.

Question 1: Making inferences

Question 1 on your exam paper will ask you to 'infer from Source A...'. There are 4 marks available for this question.

Source A: A CCP propaganda image from the 1960s that was accompanied by a caption saying 'Words of Mao Like the Power of the Sun'.

Making inferences from a source

Making inferences means working something out that isn't directly shown. First of all, think about what is suggested or implied by the source and then try to show how the source helped you make that inference. Include supporting details from the source to back up what you say.

Worked example

Give **two** things you can infer from Source A about propaganda in Mao's China.

Complete the table below to explain your answer

(4 marks)

 **Links**   You can revise propaganda and the 'cult of Mao' on page 25.

Sample answer

(i) What I can infer:
The CCP wanted Chinese people to see Mao as being like a god or super-being who always knew what was best for China.
Details in the source that tell me this:
The caption for the image says that Mao's words are like the power of the sun, and the image suggests Mao's 'Little Red Book' giving off rays like the sun.
(ii) What I can infer:
That the PLA were important in spreading Mao's message to the Chinese people.
Details in the source that tell me this:
A PLA soldier is shown holding up Mao's 'Little Red Book' so that its message shines down onto the flowers, which represent the Chinese people. The 'Little Red Book' was first developed for the PLA and it was seen as ideologically pure.

You must consider the intended **audience** and the **purpose** for which the source was produced. Also, think about **when** it was produced as this context is vital for analysing the source, not just describing it.

Sometimes, it is helpful to think about what you can see and then move on to think about what it **suggests**. You need to make sure that you don't just describe the source but go further and show you can make **inferences**.

Question 2: Explaining causes

Question 2 on your exam paper will ask you to 'Explain why ...'. There are 12 marks available for this question.

Worked example

Explain why the Guomindang (GMD) lost the Chinese Civil War (1945–49).   **(12 marks)**

You may use the following in your answer:

- the Huai-Hai Campaign 1948–49
- peasant support.

You **must** also use information of your own.

Explaining key features and causes

Explaining why involves looking at the key features of something and thinking about its causes. Key features are accurate and relevant knowledge. Causes are what led to a situation or change happening. To explain causes, you must show how a number of causes led to that event or change.

 Links You can revise reasons for the outcome of the Civil War on page 2.

You **must** use your own knowledge. Do not limit yourself to the bullet points.

Sample extract

The Huai-Hai campaign was the last major battle of the Civil War. It happened from 6 November 1948 through to 10 January 1949.

The GMD had 800000 troops, while the PLA had 600000 troops but also 600000 guerrilla fighters and peasant support.

The student clearly knows a lot about the Huai-Hai campaign and has included excellent detail about two features of the campaign.

However, the student does not explain how the Huai-Hai campaign is linked to the main focus of the question – **why** the GMD lost the Civil War.

Improved extract

Huai-Hai was a turning point in the Civil War because it was a crushing defeat for the GMD that opened the way for the PLA to invade southern China and win the war. Even though the GMD had 800000 troops and the PLA only 600000 troops, the PLA had support from peasants and guerrilla fighters, which meant it could eventually win this long campaign.

Peasant support was essential to Mao's guerrilla war tactics against the GMD, and the GMD's failure to win their support was an important reason why they lost the war. Peasants helped transport PLA equipment through the countryside. Peasants also volunteered to fight for the PLA, which boosted the PLA's numbers. This all happened because Mao promised them land reform.

GMD weaknesses were also important. For example, peasants were keen to support the PLA against the GMD because the GMD supported landlords and opposed land reform. Corruption in the GMD government was also very unpopular and their economic policies failed to control unemployment or inflation.

Make sure you identify **reasons** that help 'explain why', rather than writing descriptions of events.

Use your **knowledge of the period** to support your answer with specific information.

 Links The information about peasant support shows use of relevant knowledge. Revise these points on page 2.

Link your answer directly to the question as this student has done, with the phrase 'an important reason why [the GMD] lost the war...'

 Using phrases like 'were also important' to add a new point is a good way of writing a clear answer.

Question 3(a): Evaluating usefulness

Question 3(a) on your exam paper will ask you to judge 'How useful are Sources B and C...?'.
There are 8 marks available for this question.

Worked example

Study Sources B and C on page 41.

How useful are Sources B and C for an enquiry into the aims of the Cultural Revolution during the period 1966–68?

Explain your answer, using Sources B and C and your knowledge of the historical context. **(8 marks)**

Judging usefulness of sources

To judge the usefulness of a source, you need to think about the enquiry question and the criteria you will use to reach your decision. You will need to consider the **provenance** of each source – its nature, origin and purpose – and whether these make the source useful or not in addressing the enquiry question.

Sample extract

Source B is useful because it is written by a leader of the Cultural Revolution during the time of the Cultural Revolution, which means it is a contemporary source. Source C is useful about the aims because it is from Chairman Mao.

 **Links** You can revise the Cultural Revolution on pages 21–24.

This answer does not do enough to develop the points it makes or link them to the question.

Improved extract

Source B is useful in understanding what the CCP saw as the aims of the Cultural Revolution in 1966 because it was written for the CCP's own magazine, the 'Red Flag', which means it expressed an official view of the CCP.

Saying that the Red Guards are 'cleaning up the muck left over by the old society' is useful because it suggests the CCP saw the aim of the Cultural Revolution in terms of the 'four olds' campaign, launched in August 1966. However, Chen Boda was a radical and this might limit the usefulness of the source because the views of other senior leaders of the CCP might have been different.

Source C is from a speech by Mao and Lin Biao from towards the end of the 'Red Terror' of the Cultural Revolution. Mao and Lin Biao made this speech in order to reprimand Red Guard leaders for going too far in their attacks and warn them that, if they continued, they would be 'encircled' and 'annihilated'. This is a very useful source for understanding how the aims of Mao changed after the Red Guards started to challenge the right of the CCP to rule China. As a speech, it does not tell us Mao's private views or those of other CCP leaders.

 A good way to assess the usefulness of a source is **NOP: nature, origin and purpose**. This answer looks mainly at origin.

Key terms

Nature – the type of source
Origin – who wrote the source
Purpose – why it was created

Use your own **historical knowledge**. Compare what you know about the topic with the ideas in the source. Remember, you are asked 'how useful...?' so talk about limitations of the source too.

 Make sure you discuss **both** sources in your answer, as this student has done.

You can mix **NOP** and your own knowledge together in your assessment. Here, the student discusses the purpose of Source C and compares it with their own knowledge. A point is also made about nature ('As a speech...') and how this limits usefulness.

Question 3(b): Identifying and explaining differences

Question 3(b) on your exam paper will ask you to identify 'the main differences between the views' in two interpretations. There are 4 marks available for this question.

Worked example

Study Interpretations 1 and 2 on page 41. They give different views about Mao's aims for the Cultural Revolution, 1966–76.

What is the main difference between these views?

Explain your answer, using details from both interpretations.   **(4 marks)**

Remember to include points from **both** interpretations. It's important to refer directly to the interpretations and include short quotations to support what you say.

Spotting and explaining differences in interpretations

An interpretation is a historian's account or explanation based on evidence. When analysing the differences between interpretations, think about the points of view the historians present. Look for the important or key differences, not just the surface details. For this question you need to spot a fundamental difference between the interpretations.

 Links For more information about the Cultural Revolution, see pages 21–24.

Sample answer

These interpretations are different because the second one explains more about the aim of getting rid of Liu Shaoqi because he was Mao's rival. The first one does not say as much about Liu Shaoqi and is more about the Politburo, which was the senior officials and leaders of the CCP.

 This answer focuses on a surface point of difference rather than something more important. A stronger answer would have picked up a more important difference between the two interpretations.

Improved answer

A main difference is that the two interpretations give different reasons for why Mao launched the Cultural Revolution. Interpretation 2 implies that the reason Mao launched the Cultural Revolution was to remove his main rival to power in the Party, Liu Shaoqi. It does this by saying that, as soon as Liu was removed in October 1968, Mao 'felt there was now little reason for the Cultural Revolution'.

Interpretation 1, however, says that Mao 'had decided to unleash' the Cultural Revolution, not only to remove Liu as a rival, but to attack the CCP itself – the Party that Mao had worked so hard to build. Interpretation 1 emphasises that even the CCP did not realise this at the time. Only some were able to see as far as the attack on Liu, and no one could believe that the Cultural Revolution was 'aimed at demolishing the Party'.

 Make sure the focus of your answer is on the **key point of difference** rather than on more minor differences.

 Use **short quotations** from the interpretations to support your analysis.

 Support your explanation with details from **both** interpretations.

 Think about the language you use in your answer. Words like 'implies' and 'emphasises' help you produce a better answer because they help to show you are analysing another person's judgement or opinion about something.

Question 3(c): Suggesting reasons for different views

Question 3(c) on your exam paper will ask you to explain why two interpretations give different views. There are 4 marks for this question.

Worked example

Suggest **one** reason why Interpretations 1 and 2 on page 41 give different views about Mao's aims for the Cultural Revolution, 1966–76.

You may use Sources B and C on page 41 to help explain your answer. **(4 marks)**

'Suggest' questions

In a question that asks you to suggest a reason, you need to offer and explain an idea about why there are differences. You need to show you understand that historical interpretations are judgements and opinions based on evidence and that, as a result, different views can exist.

You must give **one** reason why historians reach different conclusions about historical questions.

🔗 **Links**   You can revise the Cultural Revolution on pages 21–24.

Sample answer

One reason why Interpretations 1 and 2 are different could be that the author of Interpretation 1 is looking at what the CCP believed at the time, while Interpretation 2 is providing a general historical view.

 This answer gives a good reason for the difference in the interpretations, but doesn't develop the answer enough.

 Answers can be developed by using details from the interpretations, your own knowledge, and/or from Sources B and C.

Improved answer

One reason why Interpretations 1 and 2 are different is that the author of Interpretation 1 is interested in identifying what the CCP believed Mao's aims to be at the time. Sources B and C show how difficult this was for CCP officials because Mao was vague about his aims, gave conflicting messages and had a past history of using campaigns to catch Party members out. As a result, CCP officials were not sure what Mao wanted. The Red Guards are praised for their actions in Source B, an official CCP source, but two years later Source C shows Lin Biao and Mao himself criticising Red Guards for going too far.

As a piece by a modern historian, Interpretation 2 is probably aiming at a general historical view, focusing on key events. It has simplified the complicated picture suggested by Sources B and C.

 Make sure you **develop** your reason, for example by referring back to Sources B and C, as this student does.

 Use your own knowledge of the **historical context**. This student does this by saying that CCP officials were not sure about the aims of the Cultural Revolution because Mao was deliberately vague about what he wanted.

 You **must** refer to **both** interpretations in your answer. You can refer to one more than the other, as the student has done here, but you must refer to them both.

Question 3(d): Evaluating interpretations

Question 3(d) on your exam paper will ask you to evaluate an interpretation by explaining how far you agree with it. There are 16 marks available for this question. An additional 4 marks are available for good spelling, punctuation and grammar (SPaG) and use of historical terminology.

Worked example

How far do you agree with Interpretation 2 on page 41 about Mao's aims for the Cultural Revolution, 1966–76?

Explain your answer, using both interpretations and your knowledge of the historical context.

(16 marks plus 4 marks for SPaG and use of specialist terminology)

 Links Find out more about the Cultural Revolution on pages 21–24.

How far do you agree?

You must:

- ✓ explore different views on the debate
- ✓ reach a clear judgement yourself
- ✓ give detailed knowledge of the context and wider issues
- ✓ use both interpretations, not just the one stated in the question
- ✓ explain your answer – develop and give reasons.

Sample extract

I agree with Interpretation 2 when it says that Liu Shaoqi was expelled from the Party and that Mao then did not think that the Cultural Revolution needed to continue anymore, because that is what happened. Interpretation 1 says that Mao aimed to make Liu less powerful, too. I don't agree with Interpretation 1 that Mao wanted to demolish the Party because Mao did not do this in the end.

The student gives a clear view, but it isn't developed or supported by evidence.

The student discusses **both** interpretations, which is good. However, more detailed explanation is needed.

Improved extract

Interpretation 2 gives a leading role to Zhou Enlai in bringing the 'disorder', which is described as 'brewing', of the Cultural Revolution to an end. It implies that Mao allowed this because the Cultural Revolution had achieved his aim of getting rid of Liu. However, in my view, this interpretation misses out the way Mao used the PLA to wind down the Cultural Revolution, with Lin Biao being very important in this.

Zhou was influential in rebuilding the Party once Mao decided the PLA was becoming too powerful, but I agree with Interpretation 1's analysis: that if anyone was controlling the chaos of the Cultural Revolution, then it was Mao. If Mao's motives seemed unclear to senior Party leaders like Zhou, then this was because Mao was waiting to see how far his purges of a bureaucratic Party system needed to go.

Analyse what the interpretation is arguing. Use quotations from the interpretation to support this.

Use your **own knowledge** to support your judgement, as the student does here.

There isn't a right or wrong answer to Question 3(d), but you must reach a **clear judgement** and **justify your views**. Make sure you refer to **both** interpretations and use your own knowledge to do this.

You need to **evaluate** different points made by the interpretations while putting your arguments into a **wider context**.

Remember that 4 marks are available for **SPaG and use of historical terminology**. Use specific historical vocabulary, such as: PLA, purges, bureaucratic.

Sources/Interpretations Booklet

These sources and interpretations are referred to in the worked examples on pages 37–40.

Source B: From a comment piece in the *Red Flag* news magazine written in September 1966. The *Red Flag* was published by the CCP and it was edited by Chen Boda, a radical leader of the Cultural Revolution.

> Coming out of their schools and into the streets, the tens of millions of Red Guards have formed an irresistible revolutionary torrent. Holding aloft the red banner of the invincible[1] thought of Mao Zedong and displaying the proletarian[2] revolutionary spirit of daring to think, to speak, to act, to break through and rise up in revolution, they are cleaning up the muck left over by the old society and sweeping away the rubbish accumulated over thousands of years of history.
>
> The Red Guards have done many good things and put forward many good suggestions… The Red Guards are the shock force of the Great Proletarian Cultural Revolution.

[1]**invincible**: unbeatable   [2]**proletarian**: workers'

Source C: Mao and Lin Biao tell Red Guard leaders off in a speech in July 1968.

> Lin Biao: You have divorced yourselves from the workers, peasants, and soldiers.
> Chairman Mao Zedong: …I think I will issue another national notice. If there is anyone who continues to violate[1] the notice, i.e. assaults the Liberation Army, destroys communications, kills people, or commits arson, he will be committing a crime. If a few people don't take the advice and insist on their line, they will be considered to be bandits, Guomindang members, and will be encircled. If they continue to resist stubbornly, we shall annihilate them.

[1]**violate**: go against

Interpretation 1: From *Mao, the man who made China* by Philip Short, published in 2017.

> At the time, the enormity of what Chairman Mao was contemplating was beyond the comprehension not only of his adversaries[1] but even of his allies. That he had decided to unleash the masses against the Party itself was too far-fetched for any in the Politburo to believe. … [Some] were beginning to understand that Mao was out to curb[2] the power of Liu Shaoqi, but saw it as part of a renewed effort to radicalise policy, not as the start of an onslaught aimed at demolishing the Party system.

[1]**adversaries**: opponents   [2]**curb**: cut back

Interpretation 2: From a piece by a present-day historian.

> As a leading member of the CCP[1], Zhou Enlai was one of those who advocated that all members of the party should be prepared to accept criticism. However, the Cultural Revolution – experimental as it was – was rapidly becoming impossible to control, and Zhou was quick to recognise this. Disorder was brewing and it was only when Zhou stressed the importance of returning to a more normal state of affairs that this threat was reduced.
>
> Many historians think that the expulsion from the CCP, in October 1968, of Liu Shaoqi marks the end of the Cultural Revolution. Mao felt there was now little reason for the Cultural Revolution: he no longer faced the menace of a rival as Liu had gone.

[1]**CCP**: Chinese Communist Party

Practice

Put your skills and knowledge into practice with the following question.

Option 32: Mao's China, 1945–76

SECTION A

Answer questions 1 and 2.

Source A: From a speech by Mao at the 1956 Congress of the Chinese Communist Party.

> In transforming China from a backwards, agricultural country into an advanced, industrialized one, we are confronted with many strenuous[1] tasks and our experience is far from being adequate. So we must be good at studying. We must be good at learning from our forerunner, the Soviet Union … We must never … become arrogant and complacent because of the victory of the revolution and some successes in the construction of the country. Every nation, big or small, has its own strong and weak points.

[1]**strenuous**: challenging

You have 1 hour 20 minutes for the **whole** of Paper 3, so you should use the time carefully to answer all the questions fully. Remember to leave 5 minutes or so to check your work when you've finished writing.

1 Give **two** things you can infer from Source A about how Mao thought China should develop.

Complete the table below to explain your answer.   **(4 marks)**

(i) What I can infer:

Guided   Mao did not think China had enough expertise to become an industrialised country.

....

....

Details in the source that tell me this:

....

....

....

(ii) What I can infer:

....

....

....

Details in the source that tell me this:

....

....

....

🔗**Links** You can revise the first Five-Year Plan (1953–57) on page 13.

Spend about 6 minutes on this answer. You need to identify **two** valid inferences from the source.

To 'infer' is to make a claim based on evidence, in this case the source you are given in the exam.

An example of a suitable inference might be that, at this point (1956), Mao still believed that China needed experts.

You need to give supporting details selected from the source to back up both your inferences.

Practice

Put your skills and knowledge into practice with the following question.

2 Explain why there was famine in China in the period 1958–62.

You may use the following in your answer:

- Bad weather in 1959–61
- The Four Pests Campaign.

You **must** also use information of your own. **(12 marks)**

Guided The great famine of 1958–62 caused at least
30 million deaths in China. Although China's leadership
blamed bad weather, this was not the most important
reason why so many millions died from starvation.

....

....

....

....

....

....

....

....

....

....

....

....

....

....

....

....

....

....

....

....

....

You have 1 hour 20 minutes for the **whole** of Paper 3, so spend about 18 minutes on this answer.

'Explain' means you have to **give reasons** for the great famine, not just describe what happened in it.

You need to include information of your own that is not in the bullet point hints.

Links You can revise the great famine and other failures of the Great Leap Forward on pages 12, 15 and 16.

Marks are awarded for your analysis and understanding of causation and for your knowledge and understanding of the topic.

Useful words and phrases to use when answering causation questions include: because, led to, resulted in, reasons for, factors that caused.

Keep your explanations focused on the question. Although you might remember lots of details about the great famine, you need to focus on talking about **reasons for** the famine, which could include Lysenkoism and backyard furnaces, for example.

Practice

Use this page to continue your answer to question 2.

....
....
....
....
....
....
....
....
....
....
....
....
....
....
....
....
....
....
....
....
....
....
....
....
....
....
....

The best answers do more than give reasons why something happened – they **analyse** those reasons. Analysing is about looking at the different parts of something to understand how the whole thing works. So, an analytical explanation looks at the **different reasons** and considers how they came together to cause something.

What different reasons have you considered for the great famine? Can you improve your answer by thinking about how they combined? One way to do this could be to talk about how natural bad weather events – droughts and floods – combined with human causes to create the famine.

Practice

Use this page to continue your answer to question 2.

....

....

....

....

....

....

....

....

....

....

....

....

....

....

....

....

....

....

....

....

....

....

....

....

....

....

....

....

....

> You should include a **conclusion** to sum up how the different causes led to this event.

Practice

Put your skills and knowledge into practice with the following question.

SECTION B

3 (a) Study Sources B and C on page 54.

How useful are Sources B and C for an enquiry into the successes and failures of the Great Leap Forward, 1958–62?

Explain your answer, using Sources B and C and your knowledge of the historical context.   **(8 marks)**

Guided Source B is useful because it suggests that in 1958 Mao saw the backyard furnaces as a success of the Great Leap Forward.

....

....

....

....

....

....

....

....

....

....

....

....

....

....

....

....

....

....

....

 You should spend about 12 minutes on this answer.

'How useful' means you have to **judge** what the sources suggest about the enquiry question and say what makes it **useful**.

Links You can revise successes and failures of the Great Leap Forward on pages 15–16.

There are different ways of analysing sources for usefulness. These include:
- considering points that the source makes
- considering **NOP** – nature, origin, purpose.

You **must** use your knowledge of the **historical context** to help you make judgements about usefulness.

You can use your knowledge of the strengths and limitations of **provenance (NOP)** to make judgements about usefulness. For example, Source B was created as propaganda, and so therefore is designed to create a particular effect by excluding other details or information. We do not see in Source B, for example, that because all the men are here at the blast furnace, important farming work is not being done in the fields.

Practice

Use this page to continue your answer to question 3(a).

....

.... ← Remember to consider **both** sources and to make a **judgement** about usefulness for both.

....

....

....

....

....

....

.... ← Focus all your points on '**how useful**' the sources are for the specific enquiry: the contextual knowledge you have (information about the period) and points about provenance (NOP).

....

....

....

....

....

....

....

.... ← Think about the strengths and limitations of different kinds of provenance. Make sure you link this to the actual sources in the question so you can use this information to judge 'how useful' they are. Avoid making general comments about provenance — **be specific**.

....

....

....

....

....

....

....

....

....

....

Practice

Put your skills and knowledge into practice with the following question.

3 (b) Study Interpretations 1 and 2 on page 55. They give different views about Mao and the successes and failures of the Great Leap Forward, 1958–62.

What is the main difference between these views?

Explain your answer, using details from both interpretations. **(4 marks)**

 You should spend about six minutes on this answer.

 You can revise successes and failures of the Great Leap Forward on page 15.

Guided The main difference is that Interpretation 1 blames Mao for coming up with the policies that caused the great famine and for deliberately ignoring evidence of the problems his policies were causing. Interpretation 2

....

....

....

....

....

....

....

....

....

You need to identify a **significant difference** in the points being made by the two interpretations, not surface differences such as what year they were published.

The question will tell you what area of the topic the difference will be about – for example, in this question, it is a difference about what was successful and what was a failure in the Great Leap Forward.

Make sure you write about **both** interpretations in your answer.

Remember, historians' interpretations are **their** views and opinions about causes, events and significance.

Practice

Put your skills and knowledge into practice with the following question.

3 (c) Suggest **one** reason why Interpretations 1 and 2 on page 55 give different views about Mao and the successes and failures of the Great Leap Forward, 1958–62.

You may use Sources B and C on page 54 to help explain your answer.   **(4 marks)**

 Guided   One reason why Interpretation 2 argues that

the policies of the Great Leap Forward were a long-term

success, instead of causing 'one of the great disasters in

history' as Interpretation 1 sees it, could be

....

....

....

....

....

....

....

....

....

 You should spend about six minutes on this answer.

 You only need to explain **one** reason, but you do need to **back up your reason** effectively, using your historical knowledge and the interpretations. You can also use the sources.

Links You can revise successes and failures of the Great Leap Forward on pages 15–16.

You can revise how to analyse interpretations on page 34. You can revise how to explain the reasons for differences between interpretations on page 39.

 Reasons for differences between interpretations can include: authors' different aims and focus; use of different sources; or because interpretations are looking at different parts of the same topic.

Remember, historians' interpretations are **their** views and opinions about causes, events and significance.

Practice

Put your skills and knowledge into practice with the following question.

Up to 4 marks of the total will be awarded for spelling, punctuation, grammar and use of specialist terminology.

3 (d) How far do you agree with Interpretation 2 on page 55 about the successes and failures of the Great Leap Forward, 1958–62?

Explain your answer, using both interpretations and your knowledge of the historical context. **(20 marks)**

Guided Interpretation 2 argues that the Great Leap

Forward was overall a success because China went on

to be very successful economically. My view of this

interpretation is

....

....

....

....

....

....

....

....

....

....

....

....

....

....

....

....

....

....

....

....

....

....

 You should spend about 30 minutes on this answer.

You can revise how to analyse and evaluate interpretations on page 34.

 Links You can revise successes and failures of the Great Leap Forward on page 15.

 You need to provide a **clear line of argument**. If you've planned out your answer before you start writing, you could say whether you agree or disagree with the interpretation in the first line of your answer.

 Say why you think the interpretation is valid or questionable.

 Review each interpretation in turn, using your **own knowledge** to analyse what they are arguing.

Keep on bringing your analysis back to how strong or weak you think each interpretation is. You must use **both interpretations** to do this, **plus** your own knowledge of the **historical context**.

 Remember that 4 marks are for **SPaG** in this question. Make sure you leave time to check your spelling, punctuation and grammar.

Practice

Use this page to continue your answer to question 3(d).

....

....

....

....

....

....

....

....

....

....

....

....

....

....

....

....

....

....

....

....

....

....

....

....

....

....

....

....

....

....

....

Remember, historians' interpretations offer **their** views for you to challenge.

Make sure you refer to **both interpretations** to back up your answer.

Include a number of **reasons** for your opinion to build an argument throughout.

Remember to use your analysis of the interpretations' strengths and weaknesses to build up your **judgement on how far** you agree.

Remember the focus of the question – in this case 'the successes and failures of the Great Leap Forward'. Your analysis and evaluation need to target that focus. Don't drift off into other reasons why the interpretations have strengths and weaknesses.

Practice

Use this page to continue your answer to question 3(d).

....

....

....

....

....

....

....

....

....

....

....

....

....

....

....

....

....

....

....

....

....

....

Practice

Practice

Use this page to continue your answer to question 3(d).

Include a brief conclusion to sum up your argument.

Sources/Interpretations Booklet 1

Sources B and C for use with the Section B questions on pages 46–53.

Source B: A propaganda poster produced in November 1958. Its caption is 'Chairman Mao visits a homemade blast furnace'.

Source C: From an article in the 'Peking Review', 8 September 1959. The 'Peking Review' was an official Chinese Communist Party publication.

> The people's commune is a powerful means for quickening the growth of our collective economy in rural areas. Since it combines industry, agriculture, trade, education and military affairs, it has certain elements of ownership by the whole people. The peasants demanded a more rational and efficient organisation of labour. This new form of social organisation was entirely the creation of the masses. During the summer this year, although the weather was bad, we got an even bigger harvest than that of 1958, the year of the Great Leap Forward.

Sources/Interpretations Booklet 2

Interpretations 1 and 2 for use with the Section B questions on pages 46–53.

Interpretation 1: From *Mao: A Very Short Introduction* by Delia Davin, published in 2013.

Mao, as the chief architect of the policies that produced the famine ..., bears responsibility for one of the greatest disasters in human history. ... In June 1959, in the midst of the disaster, Mao left Beijing to inspect conditions in the provinces. ... Reports of these talks show that he must have had some insight into what was going on. He chided[1] officials who gave him favourable reports of agricultural production, telling them not to exaggerate. In the evening the villagers complained to him that production was down and that they had had to give up their pots and pans to the backyard furnaces.

[1]**chided**: told off

Interpretation 2: From an article 'Did Mao Really Kill Millions in the Great Leap Forward?' by Joseph Ball. This article was published in 2006.

The so-called "backyard steel furnaces," where peasants tried to produce steel in small rural foundries, became infamous for the low quality of the steel they produced. But they were as much about training the peasants in the ways of industrial production as they were about generating steel for China's industry. It's worth remembering that the "leaps" Mao used to talk about the most were not leaps in the quantities of goods being produced but leaps in people's consciousness and understanding. Mistakes were made and many must have been demoralized when they realized that some of the results of the Leap had been disappointing. But the success of the Chinese economy in years to come shows that not all its lessons were wasted.

Answers

Where an exemplar answer has been provided, it does not necessarily represent the only correct response. In most cases there are a range of responses that can gain full marks.

SUBJECT CONTENT

Establishing communist rule, 1945–59

The Civil War, 1945–49

1. China in 1945

- The USA was worried about the growing strength of the USSR. It did not want China to become a communist country too, in case this made the USSR stronger.
- During the Second World War (which ended in 1945), China had been invaded by Japan. As the USA was Japan's enemy, and the GMD were the official Chinese government, the USA sent aid to the Chinese government.
- The USA wanted a government in China that would be friendly towards the USA and capitalism, to counter the USSR, so they could work to help each other's interests.

2. The Civil War

Reasons could include:

- Mao's military leadership – his strategy of pulling back his troops, when the GMD were taking control of Manchuria, reduced PLA losses. His promotion of guerilla tactics meant untrained peasants could still have a significant impact on trained and well-equipped GMD soldiers.
- Mao's leadership on the importance of the peasants – Mao believed that, if China's enormous peasant population could be mobilised, China could do anything. This belief made him help peasants with land reform and try to ensure the PLA treated peasants well. In return, the peasants backed the CCP and opposed the GMD, who blocked land reform and were associated with hated landlords. This peasant support was very important in PLA victories – for example, Huai-Hai.
- Mao worked well with the PLA generals, while Chiang clashed with some of his military leaders. This was important because it meant the PLA worked together for the same aims, instead of causing confusion.

Communist rule

3. Mao Zedong

In Marxism, urban workers rise up against capitalist bosses who exploit them and take control. This leads to a communist society in which no one is exploited and everyone works for the benefit of everyone else. The problem for China was that it had very few urban workers – 80 per cent of its population were peasants. Marx did not believe that peasants could be revolutionary because all that peasants wanted was to own their own land. Once they had that, they would become farmers and capitalists. Mao's view was that peasants could be revolutionary if they could see how they would benefit from the revolution.

4. The CCP

Mao Zedong was the president of the PRC, which made him head of state and head of the armed forces. He was chairman of the CCP, which put him in ultimate control of the Party. He selected senior party members for election to the Politburo and Standing Committee. As head of the PLA, he decided who the senior generals should be.

Zhou Enlai was premier of the State Council – the decision-making part of the government. He was a senior member of the CCP's Standing Committee, and was responsible for making sure Party policy was carried out in government.

Liu Shaoqi was the first chairman of the Standing Committee, the committee of the top leaders of the CCP. The Standing Committee was very powerful: its few members could make decisions which became law in China. Although the chairman was therefore very powerful, Mao was able to stop the Committee from meeting if he wanted to make decisions without it.

The CCP, 1951–52

5. The use of terror

CCP leaders saw the use of punishment as 'educational' because people would learn, from seeing others being punished, that they should not act against the CCP. Mao's desire to make the terror into a mass movement made sure that the terror was public, attracting huge crowds. He encouraged ordinary people to take part to make sure they identified with the state and against enemies of the PRC. This made them part of the revolution.

6. The 'antis' movements

Any two from:

- Removing people who used to be GMD meant they could be replaced by loyal CCP members who would follow Mao.
- Fining big businesses brought more money into the government, which could then be used to deliver Mao's policies.
- Both 'antis' movements targeted China's traditional bureaucracy and cleared the way for a new generation of Mao supporters to take control of government.
- Mao used the campaigns to keep his Party rivals on their toes, and make sure he stayed on top. No one could ever be quite sure how far Mao would allow the campaigns to go.

The Hundred Flowers campaign, 1956–57

7. Hundred Flowers: reasons

1 The slogan meant that Mao wanted to encourage different ideas and different ways of doing things to be discussed, so that the best ways could be identified and followed, and obstacles to progress eliminated.

2 Points could include two from:

- The Hundred Flowers campaign followed strikes in 1956. It could be argued that the campaign was a way of trying to prevent more strikes from happening by promising greater freedoms.
- There is the possibility that Mao planned the campaign as a trap to catch opponents of the regime: he never intended to allow freer speech and expression in China.
- The Hundred Flowers campaign could also have been designed to boost China's industrialisation.

8. Hundred Flowers: features and results

1 The 'poisonous weeds' were those who went too far in their criticism and revealed themselves to be working against the revolution.

2 Three ways could include:
- Zhou Enlai's apology, which weakened Zhou as a possible rival to Mao.
- Rather than thinking Mao had made a mistake by launching the campaign, people assumed he had intended to trap counter-revolutionaries all along.
- The launch of another wave of terror – the 'Anti-Rightist' purge – made further criticism of CCP rule and Mao's leadership less likely.

Economic policy, 1949–65

Agricultural changes, 1949–57

9. Land reform

Any three from:
- Land reform was very popular with peasants and, because it was the CCP that encouraged it, they supported the CCP's control of the PRC.
- Mao and the CCP wanted to get rid of the landlords as they were 'Black Category' suspected counter-revolutionaries: peasants responded very enthusiastically, and violently, to this.
- Land reform was politically difficult, but the use of terror ensured the CCP succeeded in getting 40 per cent of farmland redistributed in two years.
- The Four Freedoms gave peasants further reasons to support land reform, which helped achieve the 15 per cent per year growth in agricultural production between 1950 and 1952: another success for the CCP.

10. Cooperation and collectivisation

Any one from:
- It was essential to keep peasant support for the CCP while it was still strengthening its control of the PRC.
- Mao wanted to avoid the failures of the USSR's forced collectivisation of peasant farming, which had led to widespread peasant resistance, famine and a huge wave of terror in the countryside.
- They believed that the benefits of cooperative, socialist agriculture would be clear to peasants, who would then choose to move towards collective farming.

The communes

11. Communal living

Features could include:
- Communes were organised on military lines into work teams and brigades. Specific tasks and targets were given to each work team.
- The adults were able to work because schools, childcare and care for the elderly were all provided.
- Everyone in the commune had access to free food and healthcare, so they could stay healthy.
- Anyone who didn't do as they were told was punished by the commune's police, which helped to keep order.

12. The great famine

Your answer will depend on your own views about causes for the great famine: what is important is that you explain why you hold this view and use evidence to back it up. For example, one way of answering this question could be:

I think Mao's decision in 1958 that anything was possible in China meant that unrealistic, foolish policies were introduced into agriculture. Chinese peasants were forced to follow them, even though experienced farmers would have known they wouldn't work. Between 1951 and 1957, crop yields grew each year because agricultural policies were designed to gradually modernise peasant farming. After 1958, crop yields declined because the CCP ordered the communes to follow unrealistic ideas – Lysenkoism – and took away any incentives for peasants to work hard. When bad weather hit farming regions, instead of local problems with food supply, the whole unrealistic agriculture system fell apart and famine broke out.

Industry, 1953–57

13. The first Five-Year Plan

Before 1953, there were no bridges over China's longest river, the Yangtze. Since the Yangtze divided north and south China, it made trade and industrial development of the country more difficult. As part of the planned improvements to infrastructure, the first Five-Year Plan included the plan to build a bridge across the Yangtze at Wuhan. Goods would no longer need to be transported over the river by ferry, removing a major obstacle to China's development.

14. Plan successes and failures

When peasants stopped farming and moved to work and live in the cities, it boosted China's economy. This is because people working in cities earned money which they spent on manufactured products, instead of making what they needed for themselves, as peasants did. This meant more money for manufacturing industries, which also needed more raw materials, and this meant more demand for the products of heavy industry.

Industry 1958–65

15. The Great Leap Forward

To support the interpretation, one of:
- Mao's belief in mass mobilisation, that nothing was impossible if the Chinese people's revolutionary spirit was powering it.
- Mao's determination to develop a truly Chinese socialism rather than following Soviet ideology.
- Mao's belief that development should be spread equally across the country rather than concentrated in industrial centres.

To counter the interpretation:
- Cuts in Soviet aid meant that a new approach to industrialisation had to be found.

16. Economic reform

Three consequences of the failure of the Great Leap Forward could include:
- As many as 40 million deaths as a result of local officials' fear of being purged if they reported bad news and Mao's refusal to accept criticism.
- The rise of Deng Xiaoping and Liu Shaoqi, who led a group of economic pragmatists in the CCP and took over the emergency response to the great famine. They then

reversed some of the more idealistic elements of Mao's agricultural and industrial policies.

- From 1960, new policies for China's economy focused on economic recovery rather than working towards ideological visions.

The Cultural Revolution and its aftermath, 1966–76

Cultural Revolution: reasons

17. The Cultural Revolution

Three ways could include:

- re-introducing private farming/allowing communes to break apart
- giving control of factories, communes and state planning to 'experts' and allowing those experts to have better standards of living than workers and peasants
- allowing the CCP to become a bureaucracy that put itself in a position of power over workers and peasants, with government officials having better standards of living than the rest of the population of the PRC.

18. Purification of communism

Mao claimed that China's culture needed to be purged of revisionist, capitalist elements. Liu and Deng's moderate group within the CCP did not challenge Mao directly. They set up a committee, called the Five Man Group, to explore whether a cultural revolution was needed – as a way of taking control of the campaign themselves. However, Mao and his allies were able to use outrage over the committee's approval of the play *Hai Rui dismissed from office* to get the committee dismissed and replaced by a group that Mao controlled. This was the Central Cultural Revolution Group.

Red Guards, Red Terror

19. Student rebellion

Any three from:

- Resentment about educational reforms. These reforms (introduced by Yang Xiu-feng in 1960) meant that CCP officials could get their children into the best schools instead of this being open to everyone, and also denied many young people access to university.
- Teachers were often very strict, stuck to traditional teaching subjects and methods, and often humiliated students in lectures and lessons. Students resented teacher arrogance and intimidating behaviour. The Cultural Revolution gave students an opportunity to get their own back against hated teachers.
- Students were inspired by the radical ideas of Mao's teaching, which were expressed clearly and simply in the 'Little Red Book'. It said that the future was theirs.
- Students from poor backgrounds had plenty to gain from supporting the Cultural Revolution. Students from better off families joined to avoid becoming targets themselves, and there was also significant peer pressure to join in.

20. Red Terror

The Red Guard groups saw themselves as the defenders of Mao against his rivals. Peng Dehuai had expressed his concerns about the Great Leap Forward to Mao. Mao saw this as criticism of his policy and evidence of Peng being a capitalist roader. Other senior CCP officials who had reversed Mao's radical, ideological campaigns after the failure of

the Great Leap Forward were also targets for attacks. Their actions were evidence of them being capitalist roaders who opposed Mao Zedong Thought.

Cultural Revolution: effects

21. Political effects

The Shanghai Commune was set up by Red Guards who saw themselves as Mao's supporters, but Mao did not want the CCP replaced by people setting up alternative city governments. The Red Guards had failed to understand that Mao was using the Cultural Revolution to purge the CCP of his rivals: he certainly did not want to give up any power to ordinary people. So, the Shanghai Commune was a threat to Mao because it challenged his determination to be in complete control of China.

22. Social and economic effects

- The government made education compulsory for five years, so more rural primary schools were opened in the years 1965–76. This meant more children in poorer areas could go to school.
- Funding for education was redistributed so that poor students in rural areas got more, while better-off students in cities got less. More poorer students were able to get a good education as a result.

Cultural Revolution: end

23. Winding down

After Lin Biao's death, Zhou Enlai led a successful campaign criticising Lin Biao and the PLA for persecuting senior CCP officials in order to gain power for themselves. This made it easier for Zhou Enlai to convince Mao to allow Deng Xiaoping back into the CCP. His experience would be important in rebuilding the power and effectiveness of the Chinese Communist Party.

24. The Gang of Four

Jiang Qing, Zhang Chunqiao and Yao Wenyuan were all members of the Central Cultural Revolution Group. Yao Wenyuan wrote the criticism of 'Hai Rui dismissed from office', which was important in kickstarting the Cultural Revolution. Jiang Qing was the person who instructed him to write it and how it should attack the play. Zhang Chunqiao and Wang Hongwen were both involved in creating and leading the Shanghai Commune, which seized power from the CCP in the government of Shanghai.

Life in Mao's China, 1949–76

Communist control

25. Propaganda and censorship

Agit-prop is a type of propaganda that is specifically designed to 'agitate' or excite people to take action in line with a propaganda message. The Red Drama Groups aimed to encourage the peasants to take action as a result of seeing the play: to seize land from landlords.

26. Thought control

The 'Up to the mountains and down to the villages' campaign of 1968 mobilised over a million young people to leave the towns and cities for lives in the countryside and remote areas of China. The link to thought control is that they were to go there to be re-educated by working as peasants and living peasant lifestyles – in this way, those from a capitalist class would learn socialist ideas. But the campaign had more practical reasons too. Mao needed to break up Red Guard groups and also to deal with rising youth unemployment after the Cultural Revolution's impact on industry.

Family life and women
27. Changes in family life

Communes wanted to reduce family commitments so that women were equally as free to work as men. This links to socialist theory where men and women are equal and women are to be freed from oppression (which includes being told they must stay at home, do housework and have children). It was not very successful in the communes in practice because men still expected wives to do housework as well as work full time. Canteens in large communes were often miles away from some family homes, and childcare facilities were poor quality. Parents did not want their children to go there because, for example, they would get ill.

28. Changes for women

Three possible answers would be:

- Women could be forced into marriage before 1949. After the Marriage Law of 1950, this became illegal.
- Before Mao's victory in the Civil War, women could not own property such as land, which meant they were dependent on men. After the Marriage Law of 1950, women had the same rights as men. During land reform, the PLA made sure women were given land redistributed from landlords.
- Before Mao's leadership, women could not divorce men, even if they were suffering domestic abuse. The Marriage Law of 1950 made it possible for women to divorce their husbands, and also made domestic abuse illegal.

Education and health
29. Changes in education

As well as promoting the cult of Lei Feng, the poster shows a girl. This suggests that the CCP wanted education to continue to improve the status of women in Chinese society and encourage women to participate in building a socialist China. The poster features chemistry equipment, suggesting that the aim was to promote scientific achievement, so China would have more scientists. The message 'Study Hard Follow Lei Feng' suggests that the aim of the poster was to inspire school students, especially girls, to take their education very seriously, as something that would help both them and their country.

30. Changes in health provision

Your answer could include the following:

- Before the barefoot doctors, rural populations had very little access to healthcare so the barefoot doctors greatly improved access. Now everyone in a commune could visit the health station for medical treatment.
- Most peasant communities did not know about sanitation, and would use human waste, for example, as manure for their crops. This risked contaminating their drinking water supply with diseases like cholera. Because barefoot doctors were trained to educate everyone in their commune about hygiene and sanitation, this knowledge was spread across China, improving health.
- Training the barefoot doctors to give vaccinations meant that each commune across China had access to vaccines that prevented people developing common and serious diseases. This would never have happened if healthcare had remained concentrated in China's major cities.

Cultural change
31. Attacks on traditional culture

Three reasons could include:

- Traditional culture was seen as an obstacle to building socialism. For example, it encouraged old ways of thinking such as that peasants were stupid rather than revolutionary.
- Traditional culture was used by the enemies of socialism to justify their exploitation of others. For example, Confucianism was used by the landlord class to justify why they were in power.
- Traditional culture oppressed some parts of society. For example, women were given a low status by traditional Chinese culture.

32. Attacks on religion

Three reasons could include:

- Religion meant people following an authority that the CCP could not control. For example, Roman Catholic Chinese followed what the pope said they should do.
- Religion was an obstacle to socialist thinking. For example, Buddhist monks lived off gifts from the people so they could devote their lives to achieving enlightenment. Since Buddhist monks did not work, they could not help build socialism.
- Religion gave people an identity that might encourage independence; for example, the Muslim Chinese of the north-west regions, or Tibetan Buddhists, once China had invaded Tibet in 1950.

PRACTICE
42. Practice

1 (i) What I can infer: Mao did not think China had enough expertise to become an industrialised country.

Details in the source that tell me this: Mao says in the source that the challenge of transforming China from a peasant country to an industrial one was very difficult and that China's 'experience is far from being adequate', which means far from being enough for the task.

(ii) What I can infer: In 1956, Mao still believed that China needed experts to help it develop, especially experts from the Soviet Union, which had already developed into an industrial socialist country.

Details in the source that tell me this: In Source A Mao says 'We must be good at learning from our forerunner, the Soviet Union'. Forerunner means that the Soviet Union has gone before China and shows the way.

43. Practice

2 Your answer should focus on an analytical explanation (where you consider different causes), backed up by accurate and relevant information. You do not have to use the information given in the bullet points in the question, but you must include information of your own.

Relevant points could include:

- There was bad weather in the period 1959–61, involving floods in some regions (Guangxi in 1959) and droughts in others (Sichuan), which did significantly reduce agricultural production.
- However, although the bad weather was the official reason given for the famine by the CCP, most historians consider man-made reasons to be key in turning bad

harvests in some regions into a colossal famine affecting most of China.

- The Four Pests Campaign (the mass extermination of 'pests' including sparrows) meant a huge increase in the insects that sparrows usually ate, including locusts. Locust swarms destroyed many crops.
- The backyard furnaces were an innovation of the Great Leap Forward, but they took workers away from farming duties, which caused production difficulties due to lack of labour power (such as during harvesting). Peasants were encouraged to melt down everything metal to make steel, which left them without important farming equipment after the steel turned out to be such low quality that it was useless.
- Lysenkoism: the pseudo-scientific ideas of Lysenko were introduced by Soviet 'experts' but simply didn't work, leading to crop failures and massive waste of labour (for example, digging ditches for deep planting of seeds).
- China continued to export grain throughout the famine, which points to a failure of the government to help its own people, contributing to or even causing the famine.

46. Practice

3(a) Your answer should explain the usefulness of both sources. Points to make could include the following:

Usefulness in terms of points taken from the source:

- Source B has a graph suggesting an increase in steel production from backyard furnaces. This would be a success of the Great Leap Forward.
- The background of Source B suggests a mountainous region. One of the aims of the Great Leap Forward was for development to occur in all areas of China, not just in big urban centres.
- Source C suggests that the CCP claimed the move to communes was demanded by the peasants themselves in order to make production more efficient.
- Source C suggests that, despite bad weather in 1959, the CCP claimed that harvests across China were even bigger than in 1958.

Usefulness in terms of provenance (NOP):

- Source B is a propaganda poster, drawn rather than photographed, which is useful in terms of the message the CCP and Mao wanted to represent but with limitations.
- Source C is from an official CCP publication, which makes it useful for understanding CCP attitudes and expectations.
- Limitations on usefulness in terms of provenance: propaganda sets out an idealised view. We do not see in Source B, for example, that because all the men are here at the blast furnace, important farming work is not being done in the fields. The nature of Source C, as an article in an official CCP publication, also limits its usefulness as a record of what was actually happening in the countryside in 1959 if that would be damaging to the Party.

Historical context you could apply for judging usefulness:

- 1959 was during the great famine. The message of Source C about bigger harvests despite bad weather needs to be judged in this context. If harvests were bigger, why were people starving to death?

- The backyard furnaces did help increase steel production, but the quality of the steel was so low that it made much of the steel useless. This affects Source B's usefulness because this suggests the backyard furnaces worked brilliantly.
- In Source B, Mao is shown visiting a commune in 1958. The historical context for this is that commune officials were frightened to reveal their problems. Perhaps Source B shows just such a visit, where everyone pretended that iron production was proceeding amazingly well.
- During the great famine, many communes broke apart as people fought to survive. This argues against the message of Source C that the peasants thought the communes were a better, more efficient way of farming and living.

48. Practice

3(b) Your answer should include details from the interpretations that back up the difference you have identified. For example:

- The main difference is that Interpretation 1 blames Mao for coming up with the policies that caused the great famine, and for deliberately ignoring evidence of the problems his policies were causing.
- Interpretation 2 says that, although the policies of the Great Leap Forward caused some 'disappointing' difficulties, Mao's policies should be seen as successes in the long term because they created the foundations for China's later economic success.

49. Practice

3(c) Your answer should include details from the interpretations to support the reasons for the difference you have identified. You can also refer to Sources B and C. Your answer may include the following points:

- Interpretation 2 may give more importance to the CCP's contemporary reports and summaries, such as Source B, which stress the achievements of the Great Leap Forward. Interpretation 1 treats these sources critically, as official propaganda looking to cover up the truth about the famine crisis.
- Interpretation 2 may be aiming to re-evaluate or question what most historians see as being the truth about the great famine, aiming instead to highlight Mao's achievements. Interpretation 1 accepts the general view of the Great Leap Forward as a failure because it caused the great famine.
- Interpretation 2 may be different because it takes a very long view of the Great Leap Forward, linking it to China's rapid economic development in the 1970s–90s. Interpretation 1 has a shorter focus, considering the details of Mao's life and evaluating his achievements and failures in that context.

50. Practice

3(d) Your answer should analyse the interpretation and then explain how far you agree, giving reasons that cover both interpretations and include your own knowledge of the historical context. Your answer may include some of the following:

Points that support the argument made in Interpretation 2:

- China did go on to be economically successful after the Great Leap Forward: from 1962 to 1965, China's economy grew at 11 per cent per year, a very rapid rate.

- By the early 1960s, farming was beginning to recover from the great famine also: grain production increased by over 60 million tonnes between 1961 and 1966.
- Mao's view was that China's strength lay in its huge population. The Great Leap Forward was a success in terms of mass mobilisation of the peasants – millions of peasants did take up the new methods of the Great Leap Forward.
- Mao's view was that how people thought was very important. For him, the enthusiasm of millions of people to join in the Great Leap Forward showed China's strength as a revolutionary socialist country.

Points that counter (argue against) the argument made in Interpretation 2 are:

- Whatever the minor successes of the Great Leap Forward, the direct result of Mao's policies was to cause, as Interpretation 1 puts it, 'one of the greatest disasters in human history'. Most historians agree that the great famine killed as many as 30 million people and argue that it was Mao's policies of the Great Leap Forward that were mainly responsible for causing this catastrophe.
- Interpretation 1 says that Mao must have been aware of the serious problems of backyard furnaces from his own visits to China's provinces, and also of the growing crisis of failing harvests in 1959. As Interpretation 1 points out, Mao criticised officials who reported bad news about the harvest. This went all the way up to Peng Dehuai, who Mao severely criticised for trying to warn him about the growing disaster in the countryside.
- The Great Leap Forward was an economic disaster. China's industrial output fell by 50 per cent. Heavy industry's output fell by 55 per cent and light industry's output fell by 30 per cent.
- Interpretation 2 argues that the Great Leap Forward contributed to an economic recovery in the 1960s. However, this point ignores the fact that this recovery followed Liu and Deng's reforms, which rejected the policies of the Great Leap Forward.

Published by Pearson Education Limited, 80 Strand, London, WC2R 0RL

www.pearsonschoolsandfecolleges.co.uk

Copies of official specifications for all Pearson qualifications may be found on the website: qualifications.pearson.com

Text and illustrations © Pearson Education Ltd 2018
Typeset and illustrated by Tech-Set Ltd
Produced by Out of House Publishing
Cover illustration by Kamae Design Ltd

The right of Rob Bircher to be identified as author of this work has been asserted by him in accordance with the Copyright, Designs and Patents Act 1988.

First published 2018

21 20
10 9 8 7 6 5 4 3

British Library Cataloguing in Publication Data
A catalogue record for this book is available from the British Library

ISBN 978 1 292 17638 3

Printed in Slovakia by Neografia

Acknowledgements
Content written by Brian Dowse, Victoria Payne and Kirsty Taylor is included.

The author and publisher would like to thank the following individuals and organisations for their kind permission to reproduce photographs:

(Key: b-bottom; c-centre; l-left; r-right; t-top)

Alamy Stock Photo: Peter Probst 3, Keren Su/China Span 7, Chronicle 30, World History Archive 31, **Chinese Posters**: International Institute of Social History (Private Collection) 54,**Getty Images**: Bettmann 25, David Pollack/Corbis Historical 29, Buyenlarge 35.

All other images © Pearson Education

Note from the publisher

1. While the publishers have made every attempt to ensure that advice on the qualifications and its assessment is accurate, the official specification and associated guidance materials are the only authoritative source of information and should always be referred to for definitive guidance. Pearson examiners have not contributed to any sections in this resource relevant to examination papers for which they have responsibility.

2. Pearson has robust editorial processes, including answer and fact checks, to ensure the accuracy of the content in this publication, and every effort is made to ensure this publication is free of errors. We are, however, only human, and occasionally errors do occur. Pearson is not liable for any misunderstandings that arise as a result of errors in this publication, but it is our priority to ensure that the content is accurate. If you spot an error, please do contact us at resourcescorrections@pearson.com so we can make sure it is corrected.